HAUNTED ETOWAH COUNTY, ALABAMA

Haunted Etowah County, Alabama

MIKE GOODSON

Haunted America

Published by Haunted America
A Division of The History Press
Charleston, SC 29403
www.historypress.net

Images courtesy of the author unless otherwise noted.

First published 2011

Manufactured in the United States

ISBN 978.1.60949.360.8

Goodson, Mike.
Haunted Etowah County, Alabama / Mike Goodson.
p. cm.
ISBN 978-1-60949-360-8
1. Ghosts--Alabama--Etowah County. I. Title.
BF1472.U6G663 2011
133.109761'67--dc23
2011026793

Notice: The information in this book is true and complete to the best of our knowledge. It is offered without guarantee on the part of the author or The History Press. The author and The History Press disclaim all liability in connection with the use of this book.

CONTENTS

ACKNOWLEDGEMENTS

A special note of thanks is extended to all who helped make this book possible. Many individuals have shared stories about ghosts and strange sightings that have occurred in the past in Etowah County and that appear in some of these pages. This book actually had its early beginnings many years ago in Alabama City when people would share ghost stories trying to send shivers through a particular young child who treasured these stories over the many years.

A great deal of gratitude goes to the *Gadsden Times*, which printed and reported many of these accounts over the many years of the twentieth century. Many of the stories, especially the ones dealing with the strange creature sightings, would have been lost if they had not been reported in the pages of the newspaper.

Another great contributing force to this publication is the Gadsden Public Library, which has preserved the local newspaper on microfilm for many years. The library has also contributed its own "ghost stories," as well as a ghost that has been reported there for many years.

Many people have shared stories, fables and legends pertaining to the strange specters walking the streets and roadways of Etowah County in earlier days from Crudup to Happy Hill and Gallant. These also include the Native American settlements of Ball Play and Turkey Town and the larger towns of Gadsden and Attalla. More and more people come up to me and want to tell stories or comment on the columns that I have written, and to each and every one I am forever in debt. A special thank-you to each and every one who has offered this amazing encouragement.

A great note of thanks is extended to the many people who have encouraged my writing over the years and the many people who have come to the history tours and ghost walks that have been conducted in downtown Gadsden the past several years.

And last, but never certainly least, a great debt is owed to the schoolchildren of Gadsden, who have accepted the history and science programs with their enthusiasm to learn and keep the history of Etowah County alive and well. This enthusiasm has helped to encourage my writings over the last fifteen years.

INTRODUCTION

Did you hear that?" In the hours around midnight, in a house that is dark and quiet, a sound is heard that awakens you from a deep sleep. Is it a prowler, someone trying to get in, or is the house just beginning to settle on its foundation from age? Could it be something as simple as this, or is it something more? There is no other sound, only silence.

As sleep begins to once again take control of the night, you hear it again. This time it appears closer, possibly in the next room. Imagination begins to take control, and a vision of a ghostly specter is conjured up in the mind's eye. "Footsteps—I know those are footsteps I hear!" The sounds of the ticking clock and those footsteps are all that are heard until fatigue takes over and sleep relieves the anxiety of the late evening.

For more than 150 years, people have come to Etowah County and Gadsden seeking employment and a better way of life. The Coosa River, its majestic riverboat trade and the giant industries that have come and gone throughout our county's history have also brought stories of the supernatural. Strange creatures in and around the river and ghostly visits from restless spirits that seem doomed to walk the streets forever have haunted Etowah County since the days following the Civil War.

Stories from the 1880s concerning the "Coosa River Sea Monster," as well as a race of giants living along the banks of the river at Whorton Bend, have come from several of Gadsden's prominent families. These stories, at first the source of ridicule, have emerged again and again throughout our history.

Other ghostly legends deal with the cemeteries that were once located in the downtown area, as well as several of the unfortunate people who have lost their lives on the streets of Gadsden. These stories are about people who have reached out from beyond the grave to help others in need. Are these ghostly reminders of spirits who refuse to rest, or are they the product of overactive imaginations? Did you hear that? Now I *know* those were footsteps!

PART I
COOSA RIVER LEGENDS

For more than 185 years, the Coosa River has brought the lifeblood into what is today known as Etowah County. While this river brought the first Native Americans to the area, and later the flatboats and steamboats, the river also brought stories of strange creatures, supernatural sightings and tales of ghosts and restless spirits haunting the area. The first sightings began in the mid-nineteenth century and, strangely enough, continue to this day.

One of the earliest sightings on the Coosa River was reported as quickly as the coming of the first steamboats in 1845. Reports of this strange creature continued for many years and actually kept people from venturing into the peaceful waters until reports of the creature were dismissed by local and state officials.

Other ghost stories pertaining to the river include a ghost ship that has been reported on the river making the weekly run from Rome, Georgia, to Gadsden, Alabama, the ghost of a "roustabout" who arrives on occasion to unload the boats at the wharf and the story of a wharf that vanished into history many years ago.

Many of the strange sightings are attributed to some of the gruesome murders and tragic accidents that have taken place in Etowah County. These intriguing stories include UFOs and cemeteries where restless spirits seem to haunt their final resting place. Several of these stories have been documented by prominent citizens and have been reported in the pages of the local newspapers.

THE SEA MONSTER OF THE COOSA

With the coming of the first travelers to the area, many strange stories have grown out of the beautiful Coosa River. The river has brought commerce to the area for more than two hundred years, with Native Americans plying the waters of the river in canoes and then the coming of flat-bottom boats and eventually the riverboats. The waters of the slow-moving river also brought stories of a strange creature known as the "Sea Monster of the Coosa."

The first sighting of this strange creature was reported in the pages of the *Gadsden Times* on June 8, 1877. Marcus Foster, a respected citizen of Gadsden, was fishing in the vicinity of Ball Play Creek when he noticed a strange commotion near the opposite bank. As Foster crossed the river to get a closer look, he was amazed to find a serpentlike creature glaring at him. This startled the fisherman to the point that he quickly paddled his boat away from it. The large creature floated silently along the bank until it slipped under the water.

Marcus Foster later told of his experience rather reluctantly. Fearing public ridicule as a drunk, he later told of his experience, with several other prominent citizens relating similar experiences. It seems that this strange creature had actually been seen as early as 1862. Judge Lemuel Standifer saw this creature near Rome, Georgia. The famed riverboat captain James M. Elliott also reported seeing a strange creature drifting slowly near Rome.

Reported sightings of this monster would emerge over the next several years from Rome, Georgia, to Wills Creek just below Gadsden, Alabama. Each sighting told of a large serpentlike creature covered with scales. This monster was reported to be fifteen to twenty feet long and covered with large fins. It would always disappear beneath the water when anyone attempted to get close to it. A group of people rafting down the river reported the same creature about two miles below Gadsden. Each time the monster was reported, it was seen for only a few minutes and then would disappear beneath the waters of the river.

An explanation for the appearance of the creature was given in 1882. A newspaper reporter saw a great disturbance in the water, and he attempted to get a closer look. A close investigation revealed a large clump of leaves and weeds thrown up from the bottom by an accumulation of gases beneath. Most people living along the banks of the Coosa River accepted this theory, and the strange sea monster of the Coosa River was never

The Coosa River flows through Etowah County. It was here where the serpent was seen on many occasions.

reported again. A side note to this strange sighting was that this creature was reportedly killed at Ten Island near Ohatchee, Alabama, a few years later. A group of people enjoying a picnic came across this strange serpent and stoned it to death.

Other strange creatures have been reported being sighted in and around the Coosa River in Etowah County. These include giant fish seen by riverboat captains and also by construction workers who were employed building the first bridges across the river, as well as the locks and dams along the river. The early divers who worked on the bridge construction and the Neely-Henry Dam at Ohatchee surfaced with stories about giant catfish as large as a man on the murky bottom of the Coosa River. Newspaper legend Will I. Martin reported in one of his many columns about a catfish being caught in the Coosa River that weighed 90 pounds! Although this is a huge fish, it is nowhere close to the state record of 111 pounds.

While reports of giant catfish have surfaced for more than one hundred years, probably the strangest and most frightening sightings have been those of the prehistoric-looking fish seen all along the Coosa River known as the Alligator gar. This fish, which resembles a saltwater barracuda, has a mouth full of razor-sharp teeth, and the fish itself can reach a length of several feet. The Alabama state record for this strange creature is just a little over 151 pounds.

One of the strangest sightings of more recent days took place last fall just after sunrise. A local fisherman was fishing from a boat near Riverview Medical Center when he noticed something "floating" about ten feet from the bank. At first it appeared to be a small log, although it disappeared as the curious fisherman approached. It reappeared a minute or so later, and upon closer investigation, it appeared to resemble a three- to four-foot-long alligator. It disappeared a second time and did not resurface. The startled fisherman was reluctant to tell his story for fear of ridicule.

For many years now, the Coosa River has produced stories of serpents, giant fish and alligators. Can an alligator actually live in the climate found here in north Alabama? Are these strange reports true or just the product of a person's imagination? These stories add much to the colorful history of the Coosa River.

LAND OF THE GIANTS

During the past 150 years, many strange events have taken place that have added much to the colorful history of Etowah County. Many unusual acts of nature have caused strange things to happen in the past one hundred years. One such event that took place in 1886 in the Southeast would be felt in Gadsden and Etowah County.

During the early days of April 1886, the southeastern states of Georgia, Alabama and Tennessee were experiencing heavier-than-usual spring rains. These torrential rains would bring heavy flooding throughout Alabama that would take a heavy toll on property and also in lives. Hundreds of cattle were lost along the Alabama and Coosa Rivers during a one-week period in April, with several people also being swept away during this disastrous flood.

The affects of the flooding would also be felt in Gadsden along the banks of the Coosa River. Rainfall of eight to twelve inches was average over the first few days of April, with the Coosa River rising a full six feet higher than it had ever been. Directly across from the city, the river would measure nearly a mile in width. The water of the Coosa was so high that a riverboat was actually tied up near the intersection of Fourth Street and Town Creek. The backwaters of the Coosa River were so high that residents in many of the low-lying areas had to be evacuated.

Etowah County was very fortunate, however, with damages from this flood estimated at only $100,000. This included a heavy loss of lumber along the riverbank in addition to crops of corn and cotton in many of the river valleys.

The flood also unearthed hundreds of relics of a former civilization at several points along the bank of the Coosa River but especially on the Green Foster place above Colonel Sam Henry's place in Whorton Bend. Colonel Henry's farm lies on the western banks of the Coosa, about seven and a half miles down the river, and was said to be one of the best in Etowah County. This farm covered about 250 acres of rich river bottom and produced good crops each year. It had been in cultivation for about fifty years by this time, and Colonel Henry prided himself in having one of the finest farms in Etowah County.

On April 12, 1886, Mr. James R. Henry, the colonel's son, went down to the farm and found that nearly the entire river bottom land had been washed away by the flood. The topsoil had been swept away to a depth of three or four feet, and of the entire 250 acres only about 40 or 50 acres were then capable of producing a crop.

Upon closer examination of the land, a startling find was made. Mr. Henry discovered that a large portion of the land had once been used as a burial place for the dead of an unusual race of people. The burial ground covered about forty acres, and many curious things were found that had been buried with the dead. At the head of every grave, a pot of earthenware was found, and many contained the ornaments and weapons of war worn by the departed in his lifetime. Knives, tomahawks, pipes and other items were found and collected by Mr. Henry, who also found a skeleton that would prove to be the most startling find of the day.

The skeleton appeared to be that of a rather enormous giant. Mr. Henry could easily place his head in its skull, and the bone was half an inch think. The thighbone was almost twenty-two inches in length, and the bone from the shoulder to the elbow measured twenty inches. When all of the bones were placed in their proper places, they showed that the owner must have been close to twelve feet tall from the top of his head to the bottom of his feet. Two or three of these enormous skeletons were found in this strange burial site. Many of these people buried here were from a prehistoric race. The skulls found here were of solid bone and were flat on the top, with no seam like that found in modern man. This led many to believe that Etowah County was once inhabited by an entirely different race of people.

The unearthing of this burial ground caused considerable excitement in the area. Colonel Henry preserved many of these artifacts for people to see.

Big Sam's Return

One of the many strange stories dealing with the Coosa River is the tale about one of the many roustabouts who worked on the steamboat landing at Gadsden during the 1880s. This has to do with a giant of a man known by all simply as "Big Sam."

Big Sam was a quiet man who lived in the vicinity of the riverboat landing on the west bank of the Coosa River. No one ever knew Sam's full name; he was simply Big Sam. He stood well over six foot six and weighed close to three hundred pounds. The only scales that could weigh this giant were the large freight scales at the wharf. Big Sam could lift a large bale of cotton by himself, and many of the other dock hands were afraid of his size and pure strength. Having Big Sam on hand made the job of unloading a steamboat quick and easy for everyone else involved.

On the days when the *Magnolia* or one of the other large steamboats made a stop in Gadsden from Rome or Green's Port, Sam was on hand to help and collect his meager wages. The steam whistle would alert the dock hands of the boat's arrival, and everyone would scurry to the wharf to help unload the cargo of goods and bales of cotton. The dock manager was always generous if the tons of cargo were loaded and unloaded quickly so the riverboats could continue to their next stop. Having a roustabout the caliber of Big Sam made these stops quick and easy.

No one ever knew much about this gentle giant, and most people rarely spoke to him except to say hi. He would come to the landing when he heard the sharp blasts from the whistle, do his job, collect his pay and disappear until the next time his talents were needed. He would always show up smoking his corncob pipe and singing his spirituals, rarely carrying on a conversation with any of the other dock workers.

On rare occasion, one of the other workers would try his hand against the giant either out of anger or simple adventure. This was usually

A riverboat being unloaded at the landing. Roustabouts were used to unload the goods here, including large bales of cotton.

answered by Sam tossing the other roustabout into the shallow water of the Coosa River. For many years Big Sam would answer the steamboat's whistle and come to help unload the cargo. Finally the day came when he quit answering the riverboat's call, and much speculation was made as to why Big Sam had stopped coming to the riverboat landing. On several occasions, curious residents searched the area around the river for his shack to see if he was okay. Eventually he was forgotten, and he faded into the history of the Coosa River.

The day came when a large cargo of cotton was arriving at Gadsden, which signified the coming of the giant cotton mill in Alabama City. The cargo needed to be unloaded in record time, and not enough dock workers could be found to complete the task. Frantically the wharf manager set out to find able-bodied men to carry this out. Returning to the landing, he found the wharf completely covered with giant cotton bales. How could this be? There were not enough hands to complete this.

The story of a quiet giant who could do the work of several roustabouts was quickly told to the wharf manager. It must have been Big Sam returning to the job he loved so well. When the other workers lined up to be paid, the new dock hand was nowhere to be found. Had Big Sam returned to the job he loved so much? If so, where had he been for so long? Whatever the reason, he had returned.

Several days later, the small shack that Big Sam called home was found, along with the remains of Big Sam, who had passed away several months before. Had Big Sam actually been dead for months? Who was the giant roustabout who had helped unload the giant bales of cotton? The remains of Big Sam were brought back to Gadsden and buried in a cemetery overlooking the Coosa River. The legend of Big Sam slowly faded into the history of Gadsden and the Coosa River.

The *Magnolia*'s Arrival

Gadsden began to grow at a fast pace during the years following the Civil War, due greatly to the commerce on the Coosa River. The river is formed at Rome, Georgia, by a junction of the Etowah and Oostanaula Rivers, which flow to Gadsden and on to Wetumpka. An important route of commerce between Rome and Green's Port, Gadsden became very busy during the late 1800s. The steamboats were a major means of transportation for both passengers and goods.

An air of excitement usually filled the city when one of the riverboats would arrive at the wharf on the west bank of the river. A variety of goods were transported between Gadsden and Rome, including thousands of bales of cotton, furniture and the latest in fashions for the local merchants. Working at the riverboat landing was a heavy job, loading and unloading the boats for the many local roustabouts.

By 1873, there were six steamers making regular trips from Rome to Gadsden and Green's Port to transport the ever-increasing volume of goods. On March 13, 1873, the beautiful *Magnolia*, constructed by the Georgia and Alabama Steamboat Company, made its maiden voyage from Rome to Gadsden.

Probably the most famous riverboat captains on the Coosa River were brothers James M. Elliott Jr. and William M. Elliott. Captain James Elliott Jr. was born November 12, 1854. He became involved with boats owned and operated by his father. Captain William Elliott was born in 1862. Like

Captain James M. Elliott Jr., shown in an early photo. He was the famed riverboat captain of the *Magnolia* and several other boats over the years.

The *Magnolia* at the wharf in Gadsden.

his father and older brother, he engaged in steamboating following his graduation from college. He was the captain of several boats, including the *Sidney P. Smith*, *Magnolia*, *Hill City* and several other boats.

The *Magnolia* was the largest and most elaborate riverboat to make the voyage from Rome to Gadsden. Captain James Elliott Jr. was well known throughout the small city of Gadsden. People would scurry to the wharf to see the steamboat dock and unload its cargo of treasures. One Gadsden resident who usually made the trip to the riverboat landing was Nena Kyle, daughter of Colonel R.B. Kyle. When the whistle announced the arrival of the *Magnolia*, Nena would take her buggy to the landing to see Captain Elliott. Captain Elliott and Nena Kyle would later marry, and Elliott would become one of Gadsden's most successful and wealthiest businessmen.

While the riverboat was the chief form of transportation during the late nineteenth century and on into the early twentieth century, with the coming of automobiles and paved roads the riverboats were practically nonexistent by the days of World War I. While the beautiful *Magnolia* was no longer making the weekly run between Rome and Gadsden, the memory of this magnificent boat would live on for many years to come.

Legend has it that in the early morning hours, just before sunrise, you can hear the blast of the *Magnolia*'s steam whistle in the distance. This was usually explained as a train whistle, although a locomotive was never coming through at the time. Is this the warning whistle of an oncoming freight train, or is this the sound of the beautiful *Magnolia* announcing its arrival at the riverboat landing on the banks of the Coosa River near Gadsden's city hall? If so, is the beautiful Nena Kyle awaiting her dashing riverboat captain at the top of the bluff overlooking the river below? This is one of the many legends surrounding the Coosa River and the many steamboats that made this weekly voyage between Gadsden and Rome.

Part II
Gadsden Ghosts

Downtown Gadsden, like most other cities and towns throughout America, has its share of legends, tales, ghosts, spirits and haunted places, as well as several haunted houses. These streets and buildings are at times visited by the spirits of the long-departed people who worked here and walked these streets many years ago. Although these names are forgotten, the tormented souls have not found rest or have found this rest and had it disturbed, forcing them to face an eternity of searching.

Many events have unfolded during Gadsden's early history that have caused many hauntings in downtown Gadsden. These include tragic accidents and random acts of violence, as well as disease, that have brought about the unfortunate and early end to life. Are some poor spirits destined to walk this earth forever in search of rest, or are these sightings only the figments of overly excited imagination? Are there actually sightings of black-clothed figures wandering these streets in search of a tunnel of light that will lead them to a time of eternal rest? Do the ghoulish figures represent unrepentant souls who have taken innocent life looking for the way to a restful sleep? Are these still walking the streets of downtown Gadsden? Do these sights and sounds remain long after these tragic events have unfolded?

The early beginnings of Gadsden actually dates back to 1840, when Gabriel Hughes, along with his wife, Asenath Hughes, bought the Riley cabin at Double Springs and moved to this area from Jacksonville. Double Springs was a small stagecoach stop on the Rome–Huntsville line. This small settlement had a post office, a general store, a school and a relay station. There were also three families living in this settlement.

When Gabriel and Asenath Hughes moved to Double Springs, they were accompanied by Gabriel's brother, Joseph. In 1842, Joseph and Gabriel Hughes began buying land from the foot of Lookout to the west bank of the Coosa. The two brothers, along with John S. Moragne and William Rhea, began surveying a new town near Double Springs. This original survey of the new town would stretch from First Street to Sixth Street and from Locust Street to Walnut Street. This original survey would cover 120 acres, with Hughes, Moragne and Rhea dividing the choice lots.

The next chapter in the founding of Gadsden would take place on July 4, 1845. On this Independence Day, the quiet morning was interrupted by the loud blast of a steam whistle from a large riverboat making its way down the Coosa River. The USM *Coosa* steamed past the small settlement of Double Springs and stopped at the newly surveyed yet unnamed town. This boat, captained by James Lafferty, would pilot the *Coosa* to a predetermined landing at the present site of the Memorial Bridge. Lafferty declined having the town named Lafferty's Landing in his honor.

The name "Gadsden" was chosen for the new town after James Gadsden, who had traveled through the area with General Andrew Jackson and was a close friend of both Moragne and the Hughes brothers. It was felt that naming the town after Gadsden would bring a major railroad through the town. James Gadsden was heavily involved with the railroads and was a proponent of a transcontinental railroad. Lots were advertised in area newspapers the following year for sale in the new town of Gadsden.

THE LADY IN BLACK

Etowah County has many valuable natural resources. Because of this, our county and the cities and towns located here have attracted many people to this area since the mid-1800s. Probably the most valuable of these is the Coosa River. This river began attracting people to this area in 1845, when Captain Lafferty piloted the first riverboat down the river from Rome, Georgia, to what would later become the city known as Gadsden.

Although the river is a valuable asset to the area, several disadvantages are also associated with this resource. The biggest of these is that, for many years, there was no way to cross the river. Several ferries began operating in the Etowah County area transporting goods and passengers across the river. For a fare, a horse and rider or a wagon could be transported across the Coosa River. These ferries were located throughout the county from Hokes Bluff to Southside. By the mid-1880s, the need was becoming greater and greater for a bridge to be constructed across the river. With the coming of the railroad to Gadsden, this problem would be met head on. The first bridge was constructed as a railroad trestle during the year 1888. Through the advancement of modern technology, this wide expanse would be bridged, joining Gadsden with points to the east. With the coming of this first bridge, the ferry would soon slowly begin to disappear.

Several problems had to be addressed in building this bridge. The first problem was the construction of rock pilings in the river to support the structure. This had to be done because the river bottom was uneven, which caused the bridge to set unevenly and off-center. The next problem was that the bridge had to allow riverboat traffic. This was solved with the center section of the bridge being mounted on a large gear that allowed the

The early railroad bridge across the Coosa River. A woman in black was seen here on many occasions.

huge middle of the bridge to turn to allow the steamboats to pass. Upon approach, the riverboats would signal with a loud blast from their whistle for the attendant to open the bridge.

With the opening of this new bridge, jobs were created for bridge attendants. An attendant was stationed at each side of the bridge to regulate the traffic across the bridge. Pedestrians, as well as horses and buggies, were allowed to use the bridge. The bridge attendants were signaled by oncoming traffic. With the coming of the first automobile to the Etowah County area, an increased flow of traffic was seen using this structure. A ramp was constructed near Cox Lake in east Gadsden for automobiles to exit the trestle. The bridge attendants lived near the bridge and worked long hours regulating the traffic over the bridge.

One story that grew from the traffic across the bridge was reported on several occasions during the years 1912 and 1913. This story was about a mysterious woman dressed in black who was seen walking back and forth across the trestle. On one occasion, this ghostlike form was seen walking toward an oncoming passenger train. The horrified bridge attendant watched the woman disappear under the wheels of the locomotive. Rushing out to the place where the woman was seen, the attendant was amazed to find nothing. This unexplained phenomenon was seen over and over again by the bridge attendants. The woman in black seemed content to walk back and forth across the Coosa River, only to disappear when she reached the other side.

By the mid-1920s, the need was being felt for a new bridge across the river. The increasing amount of automobile traffic led to the construction of the beautiful Memorial Bridge. When this new bridge was constructed, the need for the bridge attendants ended. The mysterious woman in black faded into the history of Etowah County.

A ONE-HORSE DRAY

The winter months of the year are usually referred to as the cold and flu season. The weather in Alabama is so unpredictable—warm one day and freezing cold the next—that it is almost impossible to shake a cold. Mothers usually cringe when a child comes in with symptoms of a cold or flu, and the warm months of spring are anxiously anticipated. The thought of a flu

This was the former site of the Kittrell Hotel. It is now a municipal trolley stop in downtown Gadsden.

epidemic is always dreaded, with precautions taken each year to eliminate this threat. This was the case in January 1883, although the particular disease was much more feared than a cold or a flu.

Gadsden was beginning to grow at a rapid rate by 1883. The small village had survived the Civil War and was beginning to take on the appearance of a major riverboat port on the Coosa River. Gadsden had also attracted several new industries, including a large iron ore furnace known as the Coosa Furnace. With the coming of more trade and industry, the need for hotels in the Gadsden area became greater. These industries and a local hotel would play major roles in the smallpox scare of 1883.

The first smallpox scare in the Gadsden area was believed to have taken place in January 1883. It was at that time that J.F. Pendergrast came to Gadsden from New Orleans, Louisiana, to build some scales for the Coosa Furnace. It was during his stay in Gadsden, while a guest at the Kittrell Hotel, that he became very ill. The Kittrell Hotel was a beautiful wooden structure on north Fourth Street that would later house Noojin's Hardware.

At first the doctors could not agree on a diagnosis, but the next day they said that he had a well-developed case of smallpox. The authorities took prompt action by quarantining the hotel, its guests and employees, together with those operating stores on the first floor. Ropes were tied around the posts that supported the second story extending out over the sidewalk, and little yellow flags were tacked up all over the place. A small pest house was built up on Lookout Mountain, but local farmers protested and burned it down.

For the first time in its history, Gadsden had compulsory smallpox vaccinations. Dr. Joseph Bevans went from home to home vaccinating whole families. Dr. Bevans was, at that time, the county health officer. Several other doctors were also busy inoculating people, and very soon there were many sore arms in the city. In those days, there were few antiseptic devices, and some suffered more from the vaccination than they would have from the disease itself. An opposition to vaccination was built up from this that lasted for many years, all because of the crude methods used. These were the best methods known to science at the time, however.

The quarantine at the hotel was a tight one. No one was allowed to enter the Kittrell Hotel, but the doctors and two nurses, one of whom was a former Confederate soldier. This nurse had contracted the disease during the Civil War, and it was felt that since he recovered from the malady he would be immune from getting smallpox a second time. Although Mr. Pendergrast received the finest care possible, he did not recover from his illness. His mother arrived at his bedside to spend the final few days with her son before his death.

During the smallpox scare, Mr. P.J. Smith, manager of the Kittrell Hotel and one of the most colorful managers Gadsden had ever known, took things in stride. He looked after his imprisoned guests in fine style and tried in every way to ease their fright. When Mr. Pendergrast died, P.J. Smith ordered a coffin and helped to lay out the dead man. He had a one-horse dray come to the front of the hotel, and then he drove the coffin to the cemetery all by himself. Pendergrast was buried at Forrest Cemetery. Wearing his familiar gray derby hat and smoking a large cigar, he drove out Broad Street to Twelfth Street and then to the cemetery on Chestnut Street, unconcerned and unafraid. P.J. Smith was the lone mourner at the grave.

Legend has it that on unseasonably warm January afternoons you can hear the sounds of the lone horse's hooves on the streets of downtown Gadsden and the song of P.J. Smith on his slow ride to Forrest Cemetery.

The Turrentine Inn

During the early days surrounding the founding of the city of Gadsden, this area was little more than a pioneer village. While Gabriel and Joseph Hughes were planning, and with Lewis Rhea and John S. Moragne surveying the city of Gadsden, a very important family was planning to make this area their home.

Daniel Clower Turrentine and his wife, Caroline Elizabeth, moved from Milledgeville, Georgia, to Dekalb County, Alabama, in 1839 to farm a large tract of land. The family moved to the area that would later become Gadsden in 1843 and built a large inn and store. This was built on the bluff overlooking the Coosa River near the landing selected by Captain James Lafferty for the *Coosa* riverboat in 1845. Six stage lines would pass this inn or hotel and tavern that was known for its excellent service and public accommodations.

In 1851, the Turrentines purchased a farm about a mile from the riverboat landing and built an imposing residence. Portions of this land would many years later become Turrentine Avenue. It was at this time that Daniel also sold the Turrentine Inn in Gadsden.

The lawn at Gadsden's city hall was once the home of the Turrentine Inn. This landmark served as a Confederate hospital during the Civil War. Several unmarked graves are rumored to be located here.

During the early 1850s, Abner W. Keeling moved to the area and purchased several hundred acres from John S. Moragne, as well as the Turrentine Inn from Tom Holloway. Abner Keeling was born in Virginia in 1798 and died here at the home of Captain Barrett in 1883 at the age of eighty-five. He first came to this section of Alabama in 1832, buying a large tract of land at what is now known as Reed's Mill in Calhoun County, where he successfully farmed until about 1850, when he sold out and came to Gadsden. After looking around for a short time, he made heavy but judicious investments in both town and country property.

Keeling bought in the early 1850s several hundred acres of land (from John S. Moragne) later known as the Paden Farm and also the entire holdings of William Fullenwider on the east side of the river—on which lands he continued the active business of farming. At about the same time, he bought the Turrentine Hotel together with several lots from various parties in that section of the town. He completely rebuilt it, adding several rooms to the hotel, and lived there with his family, continuing to run the place as a hotel until Captain J.T. Barrett took over in 1865. In the meantime, it continued to be the stopping place for the stage line between Jacksonville and Guntersville, on which there was heavy travel—a relay of horses also being made at this point.

Early after the Civil War, Abner W. Keeling divided his vast estate, giving Ed M. Keeling his Fullenwider farms. He gave to his daughter, Laura A. Keeling, all of his town holdings, including the Turrentine Inn and the block on which it was built, as well as several other lots.

Laura Barrett was born in 1847 and received a large part of her preparatory education here under Professor John T. Slack, finishing at Mary Sharp College in Winchester, Tennessee. She was married to Captain J.T. Barrett in 1864, and together they raise five girls and two boys who were much loved and admired in their community.

Throughout the days of the late 1800s, the Turrentine Inn—or Barrett House, as it was later called—was an important stop on the line between Jacksonville and Guntersville. Weary travelers would stop at this early tavern and hotel for a meal while on a long stage journey. For many years this hotel, one of the earliest businesses in the city of Gadsden and first hotel in this area, was very popular. The Turrentine Inn would be a downtown Gadsden landmark for many years. This beautiful structure, which was located near the intersection of First Street and Broad Street, was torn down during the early 1920s to make way for new places of business. This hotel, which was built by one of the early builders of our city, faded into the history of

Gadsden after eighty years. Fortunately, some old photographs, as well as a good deal of the history of the families who built and ran this early hotel, have endured throughout history.

The days of the Civil War saw the inn used as a Confederate hospital for a period of time. Operating conditions here were very primitive at best, and the building was said to be haunted by the spirits of some of the dying soldiers. For many years the cries of the suffering could be heard in the hallways.

Today, the property where this early hotel and hospital was located is near the present site of the University of Alabama, Gadsden Center and the Gadsden City Hall. An early cemetery dating back to the Civil War was also located here. Strange sights and sounds are still associated with this eerie property. Could these be the mournful cries of wounded Confederate soldiers awaiting their meeting with the Grim Reaper?

The Haunted Jail

The original Etowah County Jail is thought to be haunted, reportedly by the ghost of Charlie Holmes, the first man to be legally executed in Etowah County. The event that led to Holmes's date with history took place on November 12, 1888. Gadsden's Deputy Marshal D.J. Kinney and another policeman happened upon Holmes while searching for another suspect. When Kinney identified himself, Holmes drew a pistol and fired once at the young Gadsden policeman, inflicting a fatal wound to the officer's side. Holmes then exchanged gunfire with the other officer before escaping to the mountains.

An enraged mob soon gathered and began searching for Holmes, determined to "string up" the murderer. After an extensive search of the mountain for several days, the manhunt was called off without turning up a trace of Holmes.

In August 1889, a former resident of Gadsden recognized Holmes in Tellico, Tennessee, although he was using the name "Charlie Johnson" at the time. After local authorities were contacted, Etowah County sheriff William Chandler made the trip to Tennessee to bring Holmes back to stand trial for the murder of Kinney. Holmes was found guilty and was sentenced to be hanged December 6, 1889. In the days before the scheduled execution, Holmes spoke freely about his crime.

The early Etowah County Jail was located on the Exchange Bank property. This was the site of Etowah County's first legal hanging.

Wade Holmes, the real name of Charlie Holmes, was born at Big Shanty, a station on the Western and Atlantic Railroad near Marietta, Georgia. He lived there with his parents until he got into some trouble about some money and was sentenced to the Georgia penitentiary. He escaped and fled to Ohio and then drifted on to Kentucky. He moved to Alabama and the Gadsden area, where he lived for almost two months before he shot and killed Kinney.

Holmes had broken into the Tolson Brothers Store a few nights before and assumed that Kinney was there to arrest him for that crime. When the police officer identified himself and began to draw his pistol, Holmes fired his own gun, killing the officer. Holmes feared for his own life and fled to the mountain. He continued along the railroad until reaching Collinsville. He would travel along the railroad until he came to a town and then would take to the mountain and travel around the town before moving back to the railroad.

Holmes soon reached Chattanooga and from there went to Memphis and on to Little Rock, Arkansas. He lived for a brief time in Texarkana and then moved on to Cincinnati and Knoxville. Holmes then moved to Tellico, Tennessee, where he felt he would be safe. This small town was fifty miles from the nearest railroad. Holmes used the aliases "Charlie Johnson" and "Charlie Franklin" while trying to evade capture.

On the morning of the execution, twenty well-armed men were stationed around the county jail. At 8:30 a.m., Holmes took a bath and donned a new suit furnished by the county. His brother, Hilliard Holmes of Georgia, had come to visit the jail at about 8:00 a.m. He was in Gadsden to take the body back to Georgia for interment. He requested a barber, and one was summoned to cut his hair and give him a final shave.

Holmes then asked for an opportunity to address the crowd in the street below. During the next ten minutes, he confessed his crime, saying that he had been an errant man and asking for forgiveness. He then said that he was thankful to God for what he had done for his soul. After addressing the crowd, Holmes was led back into the jail to the waiting gallows.

For many years after this hanging, people reported hearing the cries of Holmes in the jail. At times, sounds were heard like the trapdoor of a gallows. These ghostly reminders vanished when the jail was torn down.

On Hallowed Ground

When the city of Gadsden was founded many years ago, all of the houses, residences and stores were built around the riverfront, and the earliest settlers had their burial ground located in a small section near the corner of what is now Broad and Fifth Streets. The old cemetery had graves in the space just east of the location of Gadsden's first city hall, and some of them actually were placed on Broad Street.

When the village of Gadsden began to grow, and a more modern town was beginning to appear and grow away from the river, this cemetery was seen as an obstacle. In 1879, the Alabama legislature passed a bill authorizing the removal of all bodies and graves to Forrest Cemetery at the west end of Chestnut Street, a section thought to be "out in the country" at that time.

With this authorization from the legislature, the city began to take up the bodies and bury them again. The contract was awarded to John Plunket, an Irishman who was a professional ditch digger. Daily, crowds gathered around him and watched him and one assistant as they dug into the earth. Some of the graves yielded bodies; from most came nothing but black dirt and a few decaying splinters of coffins. It was reported that in one grave was found the body of a young soldier, almost perfectly preserved, uniform

The property that was the site of Gadsden's first city hall was once the site of the city cemetery.

and all. In another was nothing but a pile of the golden blonde hair of a young girl.

While it was not known that the old cemetery extended across Locust Street, several years later some graves were unearthed in Fifth Street when a big drainage ditch was cut on the east side of the street. Plunket and his assistant used small black coffins for removing the remains to Forrest Cemetery, which at one time had been the chief burial ground in the city and was regarded as one of the most beautiful in the country. A local legend grew from this monumental task, one that has endured for many years.

With the need for this property growing each day, the professional digger and his assistant were under immense pressure to complete this job. Legend has it that only the headstones and footstones actually were removed from the site. Many tombstones were found in a gully at the present site of Bay Street, and many residents claim that Plunket dumped them there to save time.

Gadsden enjoyed many improvements in 1904. One of the major problems with city government was addressed in April 1904. A seat for city government had become a necessity, and the first Gadsden City Hall was built on North Fifth Street.

City hall was completed late the following year, and the city's offices were consolidated. The fire department was now located at city hall, as was the police department. The mayor's office was relocated to the new municipal building. A beautiful dome crowned this structure, which served as the center of city government for the next fifty-six years.

Today, much of the property that once was the home of the city cemetery is a parking lot. The original city hall was torn down during the 1960s and has been paved over. Many people have forgotten about this early cemetery, as well as the legends of the graves there.

A Distant Drummer

Most downtowns have their haunted buildings. These structures are intriguing and have colorful pasts. Many buildings were the scenes of tragic events or disastrous fires of legendary proportions. Such was the case of Gadsden's Printup Hotel, which is recognized as one of Gadsden's most haunted structures. This grand hotel was dedicated on July 6, 1888, and had a colorful history. The hotel became a favorite stopping point for many travelers and visiting dignitaries.

The Printup Hotel was patterned after the famed Kimball House in Atlanta, Georgia. The four-story structure was capped with a towering dome used as a skylight. The second floor of the hotel housed the kitchen and an elaborate dining room. The first-floor lobby was complete in every manner, including a railroad ticket office to serve passengers who wished to arrive or leave by train. Passenger trains made regular stops at the Locust Street entrance to the hotel.

During the early years of the twentieth century, many famous guests visited the Printup Hotel. Clarence Darrow, the famous criminal lawyer from Chicago, stayed at the hotel while on a tour of the South during Al Smith's presidential campaign. William Jennings Bryan, the famed orator, also spent a night at the hotel while on a visit to Gadsden.

Under the management of the Adolph Reich family, this grand hotel flourished during the early decades of the twentieth century. The Printup was modernized and redecorated while owned by Reich. In 1925, a small

The Printup Hotel was reported to be haunted. People working in this building in recent years have reported strange sights and sounds in the hallways.

fire broke out in one of the rooms. Although the fire damage was slight, the hotel suffered extensive water damage. The hotel was redecorated, with the same decorating scheme being used.

In February 1929, a late-night fire broke out in a room on the third floor. This fire caused extensive damage to the third and fourth floors. This spectacular fire was not contained until the following morning, with the embers smoldering for many days following.

The management of the hotel once again undertook a major renovation of the structure. The fourth floor, with its majestic dome, was removed during this renovation. The owners practically tore the hotel down and rebuilt it with steel and concrete, making it as fireproof as possible. For many years, the elegant beauty of the Printup Hotel entertained many visitors to the Gadsden and Etowah County area. This beautiful landmark went through many changes, although it continued to be the center of many important events in Gadsden's early history.

An event that took place in the grand hotel's past that brought the first mention of ghosts began during the time of the open saloon in downtown Gadsden. The major saloon district was in the 400 block of Broad Street adjacent to the early Etowah County Courthouse. A "drummer," or traveling salesman, was in town to call on perspective customers in the area. On this occasion, the drummer was experiencing a successful stop, and his sales reflected this success. Following a record day of sales, the drummer stopped at one of the local saloons and was flashing a rather large roll of currency for everyone to see. This would prove to be a very grave mistake.

Someone followed the traveling salesman back to the Printup Hotel and up to his room on the fourth floor. This was on a Saturday night, and if anyone heard the gruesome sounds of what transpired over the next few moments, they either chose not to get involved or the small police department never received the call for help. The crime would not be discovered nor reported until the following morning. The early hours of dawn produced a crime scene that was almost too horrible to imagine.

Because the drummer was not seen the following morning calling on his prospective customers, the management of the Printup feared that the hotel guest had simply skipped out without paying his bill. As the day went on, the hotel manager and town marshal reached the decision to enter the room. They found the body of the traveling salesman on his bed. He had been badly beaten, and his throat had been slashed. The strange thing was that no one reported hearing anything out of the ordinary the night before.

Robbery was the obvious motive for the crime. The large amount of cash was never found, and no witnesses ever came forth to tell of any sights or sounds of the murder. The case was soon closed because of a lack of evidence. Although the case was officially over, this was just the beginning of the strange occurrences at the Printup Hotel.

The sounds of a brutal murder were reported on many occasions on the fourth floor of this beautiful structure. Footsteps could also be heard in the hallways, although no one would ever be seen walking there. Voices could also be heard in the different rooms on this top floor. The strange sounds and feelings that were heard and felt in this room were so strong that no one would stay the night there. As the years slowly went by, the history of this room slowly faded into the history of Gadsden and Etowah County.

As the years passed by and travelers arrived by train at the Printup, people would be given the key to this fateful room, although the strange occurrences always caused people to ask for another room. After the fire of 1929, the fourth floor was torn off, eliminating the haunting sounds of the crime that took place there, or so everyone thought. On many occasions,

One of the destructive fires at the Printup. The fourth floor was removed after this fire.

lights have been seen coming on and going off at strange hours of the night and early hours of the morning.

From its early days, the Printup Hotel has been the home of many business establishments. Barbershops, beauty parlors, restaurants and other places of business have called this historic building home. Recently a former employee of one of these businesses reported strange sights and sounds from the upper floors, as well as the uncomfortable feelings that caused most of the employees to hurry to their cars at quitting time.

Today this building has been renovated and sits quietly on the corner of Fourth and Locust Streets, a quiet testimony to the history of more than one hundred years of downtown Gadsden. This beautiful hotel building that welcomed prominent visitors to Gadsden, including William Jennings Bryan, and was the site of many important announcements concerning Etowah County's future is today a private business establishment. Does the "drummer" come back on occasion looking for the large roll of bills that he was carrying on this fateful night more than a century ago, or are all of these events only the figments of the imagination?

The Curious Ghost

Downtown Gadsden has had its share of ghost stories and tales of unusual sights and sounds. The early days of the twentieth century saw the small town beginning to grow into a modern city. Several destructive fires of the nineteenth century helped the downtown area progress from a dirt street lined with wood-frame storefronts to a modern town with brick-paved roads and brick storefronts.

One Fourth of July celebration that will be remembered throughout the history of Gadsden was the one that took place in 1883. This Independence Day started with many gala events and ended with the downtown business district of Gadsden being almost totally destroyed. Many northeast Alabamians had made the trip to Gadsden to attend a horse-swapper's convention and had stayed to participate in the patriotic activities planned throughout the day.

After the horses had been displayed, a colorful military parade was staged by the Etowah Rifles, a local home-guard unit. This parade ended at the Etowah County Courthouse. Following the parade, Colonel William H. Denson began a speech that would come to an abrupt halt one hour later. It was at that time that the bell from the fire station began to sound an alarm for the small Gadsden Fire Department to swing into action. What unfolded in the next few hours almost spelled doom for the town.

A fire had broken out at the residence of Ben Whorton, who lived at the corner of Third and Broad Streets. Efforts to bring this fire under control were hampered by the fact that an extremely high westerly wind was blowing that day. Another issue was the fact that most of the buildings on Broad Street at this time were wooden structures. The small fire department, which was mainly a "bucket brigade," fought gallantly, although they were hindered by many of the intoxicated horse swappers.

This fire burned out of control until it reached the brick walls of the Kyle Opera House located in the 400 block of Broad Street. In all, twenty-six businesses were destroyed, with an estimated value of more than $100,000. The Etowah Rifles stood guard throughout the night to keep looters from pilfering through the burned-out stores. This spectacular fire destroyed many businesses, although brick buildings were soon built to take their place. Today, many of these buildings that grew from the smoldering ruins of this great fire are still standing.

Little Faces Doll Shop was once the home of Mitchell Brothers Saloon. Strange sounds are still heard here on a regular basis.

During the late 1800s and early 1900s, many saloons lined Broad Street in the 400 block. These businesses were very popular with many of the men working in the downtown Gadsden area, especially at Kyle's Sawmill and the other industries there. Spoon Motlow's Saloon was popular in the Gadsden saloon district, as well as Mitchell Brother's Saloon located across from the Etowah County Courthouse. Although these places were popular, the clientele was composed of extremely rough characters, and by the early days of the twentieth century, many felt a great need to see the open saloon era come to a close. Other saloons at this time included Bill Echols' Saloon in Gadsden and also Nugent's Saloon in Attalla. Gadsden also had a crockery industry at that time, and the different saloons had their own jugs made with the saloon's name cut into the crockery.

In late 1906, Etowah County citizens voted to dry up the county, thus ending legal distilling by early 1907. Spoon Motlow would soon leave Gadsden and return to Tennessee to continue in the whiskey business. As time progressed, these buildings that were once the home to these saloons or "watering holes" have been transformed into a wide variety of stores. These storefronts made up the downtown business district of the 1950s until the 1970s, when many shopping centers and malls opened in the Etowah County area.

Today the building that once housed Mitchell Brother's Saloon is now the home of Little Faces Doll Shop, which is a specialty shop that sells dolls and actually handles doll adoptions where children adopt these very lifelike creations. One feature of this shop is the nursery that covers the back of the store. When the doll shop opened in this location, strange occurrences began almost immediately. The first unusual event that took place here began shortly after the building was renovated. The storefront was changed, and the tile floor was removed, including at the entranceway that said "Mitchell Brothers Saloon."

Soon after this renovation, the first "sounds" were heard in the walls and upstairs. These have never appeared to sound like voices but rather things being moved or footsteps on the upper floors. With the passing of time, these sounds have become an everyday thing and go by almost unnoticed. These, however, were only be the beginning of the unusual things seen and heard here. One of the most remarkable sightings in this store is a plate holder that hangs on the wall in the nursery. At any given time, this holder can be seen swinging from side to side for no apparent reason. Things in the nursery would be quiet and still, and this wall hanging will begin swinging from side

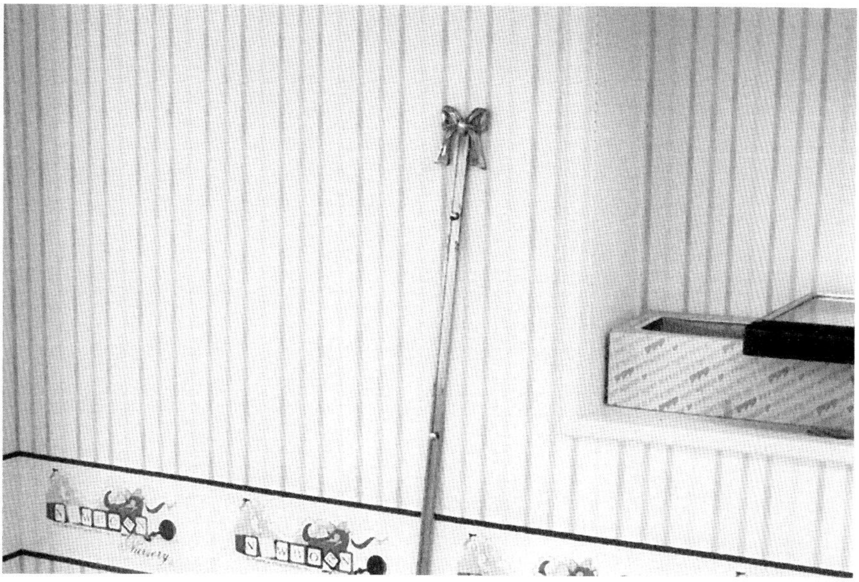

Things move at times for no apparent reason, such as this plate rack located in the nursery.

to side. One apparent explanation was that this was hanging near an air conditioner vent, although after being moved it would begin moving once again on its own.

Another strange occurrence here has to do with images and orbs of light that have been captured on digital photography. Many photos have been taken here as the dolls are adopted, with nothing appearing on the photograph; then a strange image will appear for no apparent reason.

While many ghosts in haunted buildings are thought to be violent, the ghosts here are very docile and curious. These strange happenings take place at unusual times, and the feeling here is not one of fear but of a peaceful coexistence with the resident ghosts. Are these ghosts former customers of this early saloon in Gadsden's history, or are they just curious onlookers fascinated by the babies in the nursery waiting to be adopted?

Gadsden's Haunted Library

One of the more prominent haunted buildings in downtown Gadsden is not one of the oldest buildings or one of the eeriest. The building where more strange sights and sounds have been experienced is the Gadsden Public Library, located on College Street. Most of the library patrons who visit this modern structure each day are probably not aware of the ghostly sightings that have been experienced on the third and fourth floors.

No one is exactly sure just when the strange sights and sounds began here. Perhaps the people who first heard or saw these ghostly apparitions were afraid of being held up to public ridicule or just dismissed these sightings as shadows or the results of an overactive imagination. Whatever the explanation, the sightings and sounds increased with the passing of time. Just where did these ghostly specters originate, and why have they appeared in a building that is relatively new compared to the other downtown structures that have had a history of paranormal events? A look at the library's history and the property's past may help to explain the sightings.

In the spring of 1897, the Thursday Study Club was organized at the home of Biancha Randall. Calling themselves the "Bachelor Girls," this group of young women originally entertained itself by playing cards. Amid objections by their parents to their activities, they adopted the title of the Young Ladies Literary Society. In 1899, the group renamed itself the Thursday Study Club and adopted a project of opening a public reading room. Several fundraisers—including theatrical productions, ice cream parties and oyster suppers—took place. In three years, the group raised $256. The club purchased a small collection of books and rented a front room in the new Moragne Building, in the 400 block of Broad Street, for six dollars per month. Club members took turns keeping the reading room open for patrons. This small reading room developed into an honored institution, and its significance in education and cultural life was recognized by leading citizens of Gadsden.

In 1904, an agreement was reached with the Carnegie Foundation for a $10,000 grant to build a public library in Gadsden. This was made possible through the efforts of Walter E. Striplin, superintendent of public schools. Striplin publicly solicited funds to purchase property on the northwest corner of Seventh Street and Forrest Avenue for the library. After the property was purchased, the Carnegie Foundation donated the funds for the construction of the library, which was formally dedicated on December 20, 1906. The

The Gadsden Public Library has been reported as being haunted for many years. A medium was brought in several years ago to explain the strange sightings here.

nucleus of the library was the small collection of books that had been purchased by the Thursday Study Club. Miss Lena Martin became the first librarian at the Gadsden Public Library.

This beautiful structure served as the main branch of the Gadsden Public Library for many years. In 1942, a large addition was completed to the Carnegie Library building. For more than twenty years, this building served as the Gadsden Public Library. This building, along with Miss Lena Martin, is still remembered by hundreds of people who frequented the Gadsden Public Library. By the early 1960s, this structure was beginning to show its age, and plans got underway to build a new structure to house the library.

In the early 1960s, Gadsden would go through a building boom. Gadsden was awarded an Accelerated Public Works Grant of $272,000 to match city money for a new library building. The new library would be built at 254 College Street on the old Striplin School property. Roberts Brothers was awarded the contract to build the new structure with a base bid of $503,331.

The new library would be ready for occupation in twelve months. The thirty-nine-thousand-square-foot structure had room for almost 200,000 books. The new Gadsden Public Library was notified that it was being designated as a federal depository for the government documents of Congressman Albert Rains.

The old Gadsden Carnegie Public Library closed its doors for the last time on May 16, 1964. The dedication of the new Gadsden Public Library was held on June 28, 1964, with Albert Rains being the featured speaker. The lecture room was furnished and dedicated to Miss Lena Martin by the Thursday Study Club. During the 1960s, the Gadsden Public Library continued to grow. The library expanded into the north Gadsden and east Gadsden areas.

It is unknown just when the strange occurrences began at the Gadsden Public Library. Strange sounds, smells and sightings were occasionally reported in the closed stacks on the third and fourth floors, although employees were hesitant to report these. At times people working in the library on Sunday afternoons, when the facility was closed, heard young children talking and at times crying, breaking the silence of a quiet afternoon. An investigation of the children's department would usually turn up nothing. These were rarely reported until the mid-1990s, when the strange sightings took an unusual twist. The next report of a ghost in the library was an actual sighting rather than sounds or odors coming from the third floor.

The first sighting of the ghost at the library took place near closing time when an employee went up to turn off the lights on the third and fourth floors. As customary, the elevator was taken to the fourth floor to shut off the lights. As the elevator doors are opened, the emergency stop is pulled out so that the elevator could not be called to one of the lower floors. The lights are then turned off and the elevator is then taken to the third floor. As the doors opened and the employee pulled the emergency stop button and began to step from the elevator, they were startled to see a woman dressed in nineteenth-century clothing looking through an old card file near the elevator doors. The startled employee looked on as the lady slowly faded away. The lights were quickly turned off, and the visibly shaken employee hurried downstairs.

This library employee witnessed the same ghostly specter on many occasions, although he was reluctant to talk about it until this account was divulged to another employee. To his surprise, this ghost had been seen by more than one employee. At times footsteps could be heard on the third and fourth floors, and the sound of muffled voices could also be heard. Also, the unmistakable smell of a coal fire could be detected on the third floor of the library. These sightings continued for several years until an unusual third party was brought in to help with these restless spirits.

A medium was contacted and traveled to Gadsden from the Mississippi area. This individual was well trained in paranormal occurrences and was readily available to offer explanations into these strange sightings. Equipped with an amulet and an orb, the medium closely examined the third and fourth floors of the library. After examining the area where the ghost was seen on several occasions, two dates were determined. Accompanied by several local historians, the medium had one move to the far corner of the room. At this time, he asked, "What do you feel?" In this particular corner, the room was much colder, and one person noticed the hair on his arms standing straight up. The medium replied, "This is an indication of a presence!"

Since its early sightings, speculation was made as to who this ghost may have been. One guess was that of Miss Lena Martin. Lena Martin was the first librarian hired by the City of Gadsden when the original library was opened on Forrest Avenue.

A search of historical records helped identify the lady and also offered several other explanations of other sounds and smells. During the 1870s, one of the earliest schools in downtown Gadsden was the Gadsden Male and Female College. An early photograph of the faculty identified the lady as Ms. Minnie Lay, a teacher at the school. The dates the medium came

The third floor, where ghosts have been seen and heard.

up with were important dates in her life. The sounds of children's voices at play were probably from the children who attended this early school. The unmistakable smell of coal burning was that of the early potbellied stoves that would have once been used to heat this old wooden structure. Although the "lady" had been identified, the strange sounds continued. Most employees seemed to be accustomed to these sounds, like a building settling on its foundation. These sounds would be ignored for the next several years.

The Gadsden Public Library underwent a major renovation a few years later, with the facility being closed for a period of time. Many things were removed from the library and stored at other sites around Gadsden. The new modern facility celebrated a second grand opening with a new look, new computers and new rooms. The only thing missing from the library were the strange sights and sounds on the third and fourth floors. Several trips have been made to these floors on occasion, including one on Halloween, with no strange sounds or sightings reported.

Have the ghosts moved on, or are they simply satisfied with their new surroundings? Whatever the case, these spirits have not been seen or heard, nor their presence felt, in several years now.

The Ghost of the Princess

Since 1906, people living in Etowah County have been fascinated by motion pictures. More than fifty theaters, large and small, have existed here for a time. Some were in operation for a short period, while others had long and colorful existences. One of Gadsden's more successful movie houses was Gadsden's beautiful Princess Theatre.

The Princess Theatre was originally known as the Imperial Theatre when it was opened on November 24, 1920. The first movie shown was *The Right to Love*, which starred Mae Murray and David Powell. A capacity crowd filled the 730 seats on opening night. The Imperial was the first real challenge to the Gadsden Theatre for the entertainment dollar in Etowah County.

In July 1926, the theater changed hands, and an extensive facelift took place, transforming the Imperial into the Princess Theatre. A balcony was added, as well as a vaudeville stage. The interior of the house was redecorated. The Princess was opened on September 11, 1926, with the movie feature

Gadsden's Princess Theatre was rumored to be haunted by the ghost of a young girl.

being *The Phantom Bullet* starring Hoot Gibson. Balloons were released on the morning of the grand opening, each with a free ticket attached.

The Princess enjoyed a long and successful life until 1937, when plans were announced to remodel and enlarge the theater. The Princess was reopened on June 17, 1937, to a huge crowd in the totally rebuilt auditorium. The opening night feature, *Woman Chases Man*, was viewed by a capacity crowd of 1,500. The Princess was said to be the last word in moving picture show houses. It had the latest equipment, and it was as comfortable as money could make it. It was air-conditioned with an eighty-ton ice machine and was heated with the most modern apparatus then known.

The 1,500 seats were unsurpassed for comfort. No seat was directly in front of another, and they were far enough apart to prevent crowding. The lighting system was the most modern known to the business and added to the attractiveness of the interior, which had been decorated by some of the best artists in New York.

There were three luxurious lounging rooms in front, two for women, and a magic eye opened the front door. Exquisite Wilton carpets covered the aisles and lobbies. The ceiling was four shades of blue and green, with aluminum trim. Heavy drapes were everywhere. The front curtain and valance were of a bright red velour.

As beautiful as this auditorium was, it had an unusual story associated with its location and the previous occupant. In 1860, Gadsden's First Baptist Church was built on this property. There was a small cemetery located behind the church, as well as the city cemetery located adjacent to the church. The church was here until 1899, when property was purchased two blocks away, and a new structure was built. Whether the graves were relocated was never known. The only thing that was certain was that many strange sights and sounds were encountered here, especially after the movie theater was built here in 1920.

Shortly after the Imperial Theatre opened, a young girl was seen in the auditorium on many occasions walking up and down the aisles or just sitting and watching the movies. This child always seemed fascinated by the organ that was played with the silent movies. This young girl was seen here on a regular basis, although no one ever saw her enter or leave the theater. The child became such a "regular" customer that the theater manager began watching for her to see if she was slipping in, although she was never caught entering or leaving. This ghostly figure never appeared to bother anyone or say anything to anyone. She appeared to be fascinated by the movies and the live shows that the Princess Theatre had to offer.

In 1947, a new theater opened on Broad Street, and a friendly rivalry broke out between the management of the Pitman Theatre and the Princess Theatre. For quite some time, the Princess Theatre had more to offer than the newer Pitman Theatre. The Princess had first-run movies, more comfortable seating and its own ghost, although this was not readily publicized. Gradually, the Pitman Theatre would reverse this trend, however. This friendly rivalry came to a fiery finish on a cold winter night in 1963.

The Princess Theatre's last movie was on November 4, 1963. Fewer than one hundred people were enjoying the movie *All the Way Home*. It ended at 10:30 p.m., and the theater closed its doors for what would be the last time. At 10:48 p.m. the night of the fire, Gadsden police officer Bill O'Bryant was walking his beat when he noticed what appeared to be a garbage can burning next to the theater. O'Bryant turned in the alarm, and several fire engines answered the call. When the first trucks arrived, they found the theater engulfed in flames. The firefighters battled the flames into the night and early morning hours. By daybreak, the once beautiful Princess Theatre had been reduced to smoldering embers.

The Princess Theatre carried only a minimal amount of insurance, and the decision was made not to rebuild the theater. The burned-out shell of the

Children loved the Princess, and it was a popular place until it burned down in late 1963. The image of the young ghost vanished after the theater was later torn down.

once beautiful movie house was torn down, and the Princess Theatre slowly faded into the history of Etowah County. Although several businesses have occupied this corner lot at Fifth and Broad Streets, the strange sightings and sounds have vanished.

Belk Hudson's Department Store was located here before eventually moving to the Gadsden Mall. After several years of being empty, the Hardin Center for Cultural Arts purchased the building. Following a major renovation, the "Center" opened amid much fanfare. The young girl who had walked the aisles and watched the movies seemed uninterested in the new occupant of the address and was never seen or heard from again.

Was this young girl a ghost of someone who had been buried in the cemetery located behind the old church on the corner or simply a spirit that was fascinated by the motion pictures of the twentieth century? Did the child haunting the Princess Theatre simply become bored with the ever-changing face of Broad Street and eventually fade into eternity? These questions will probably never find an answer.

The Ghost of the Trestle

For quite some time, a move has been underway to get the railroad bridge that spans the Coosa River at Gadsden repainted and refurbished. This huge steel structure had appeared rusted and dilapidated and almost looked to be a hazard for the many trains that use it daily.

For many years, this historic structure was the only traffic bridge in the area. During this time, the only way to cross the Coosa River at Gadsden was by using one of the many ferryboats. The problem was addressed in the late 1880s when a railroad trestle was built that also was used for horses and wagons and, later, automobile traffic.

The old bridge across the Coosa River in Gadsden was closed to everything except for railroad traffic at 1:00 p.m. on Monday, June 28, 1909. All vehicles and pedestrians were ferried across the river. The ferry, which operated by steam cable, was in service and was making round trips in ten minutes. The service was as good as it could be under the circumstances, and the ferry could handle nearly as much traffic as what traveled across the railroad bridge. A number of farmers were using the public ferries above and below the city.

On the morning of June 29, a large force of men was put to work ripping up the flooring of the old bridge. When the plank flooring was torn away, huge pile drivers were moved onto the structure to drive the piles for a false structure over which the trains would run when the old steel spans were lifted away. The piles were driven into the bed of the stream. As soon as the timbers were placed and the steel structure removed, work began on the piers. The wooden bridge was used until the new steel one was ready to be set on the rebuilt piers.

It was anticipated that the bridge would be completed in only five months. The new railroad bridge would be the heaviest one of its kind in Alabama and was made necessary by the immense and ever-increasing traffic across the Louisville and Nashville Bridge.

By mid-November, the new bridge was nearing completion when a tragedy occurred. A twenty-one-year-old Gadsden resident, a well-known young man, fell from the Louisville and Nashville River Bridge at 2:40 a.m. and was killed instantly. His remains were shipped to Spring Junction for burial.

The victim was working on the new bridge at the time of his death. The bridge had electric lights strung across the structure and had both day and

The L&N railroad trestle was reported haunted by several ghosts, including the specter of a worker killed here when the bridge was rebuilt.

night crews working. He was a member of the night crew and was engaged in unloading a car of concrete. The concrete was being taken from a railroad car on top of the bridge and sent down a gangway in wheelbarrows to the central pier, which was being rebuilt. The worker was rolling one of these wheelbarrows and lost his balance. He fell clear of the trestlework to the old cofferdam at the bottom of the pier, striking on a pile of rocks. When his fellow workers reached him, he was lifeless. His left leg and jaw were broken, and he had a severe gash on his head. His body was badly bruised after falling about seventy-five feet.

The Woodliff and Dunlap ambulance was summoned, and the body was carried to its undertaking establishment and prepared for burial. Miller was unmarried. He was the son of John Miller, the watchman at the bridge. The new Louisville and Nashville Bridge was completed a short time later without any other mishaps. It was the only bridge across the Coosa River at Gadsden until 1927, when the Memorial Bridge was constructed.

Shortly after the railroad bridge was reopened, the strange sights and sounds began. At times, an unusual ghostly light was seen around the middle span of the bridge just above the surface of the river. At other times, a faint sobbing was heard by people walking across the railroad bridge from east

Gadsden to Gadsden. These sounds were so eerie that pedestrians began to avoid the railroad bridge at night. These experiences continued until 1927, when the new Memorial Bridge was built for automobile and pedestrian traffic. With the opening of this new bridge, the ghost of the railroad bridge soon was forgotten.

Recently, a facelift and refurbishing began on this old steel bridge. The structure has acquired a fresh coat of paint, and the bridge looks almost new. With this new look coming to the old bridge, perhaps the specter that was once seen and heard here will one day return.

The Electric Park

People living throughout the Etowah County area have looked for ways to beat the heat during the long hot days of summer. Early Etowah County residents took comfort in the cool surroundings of Noccalula Falls and the nearby caves and springs. This was a popular tourist attraction for many sightseers who took the riverboats from Rome to Gadsden. By the early 1920s, a new form of entertainment had begun to take the county by storm. These attractions were in the form of amusement parks that featured a large swimming pool.

Several of these parks in the area during the 1920s would be in existence for many years, while some would fade into history after only a few years. Some of these early lakes in the area included Hooks Lake in north Gadsden, Lake Rhea in Attalla, Anderson's Lake in Glencoe and Rainbow Lake in Gadsden. Anderson's Lake was a popular place on opening day, May 29, 1926, and Lake Rhea was a favorite as far back as 1925. Rainbow Lake was located in west Gadsden near Black Creek and advertised the most sanitary swimming conditions of 1927. One lake that was a favorite of many living in the Gadsden area was known in its early days simply as the Electric Park.

The Electric Park was one of the most popular amusement parks in Gadsden during the 1920s and early 1930s. During the 1920s, this area was accessed from a road near the end of old South Fourth Street. A dirt road led from Fourth Street past a swampy area located where the Gadsden Mall is today and on to the Electric Park. This was long before Rainbow Drive came through the area.

The overgrown remains of the Electric Park. The walls of the swimming pool remain, although they are hidden from view by years of growth.

The Electric Park quickly became a favorite place for the young people to go during the hot days of summer. The trip from downtown Gadsden did not seem too long to most of the youngsters going down to enjoy the amusements at this park. A large swimming pool was located here, with clean, fresh water added daily. There were also several amusement rides located here, as well as a skating pavilion. Bowling was also offered at the Electric Park, as was as a shooting gallery. A person could go to the gallery and try his skill at shooting .22-caliber rifles. A bus ran from downtown Gadsden to the park. People could catch this bus on the corner of Third and Broad Streets and ride to and from the park.

In 1928, the park became known as the Rainbow Electric Park, after it combined names. Several new attractions were added to the park, as well as a large dance floor. A dance was held here each Thursday night that quickly became a popular attraction. Under the management of W.M. Smith, the Rainbow Park continued to grow in popularity. On one occasion, Jack Linx brought his famous orchestra from Birmingham to play at one of these dances. Admission to this dance was $1.50. On another occasion, Dayton Howard brought his jazz orchestra to the park to entertain.

For several years, the Electric Park, or Rainbow Park, was one of the most popular amusement attractions in this area. At a time when competition was keen for the entertainment dollar, the Electric Park flourished. Competition with the other lakes in the area, as well as the movie theaters such as the Belle, Princess and Lyric, kept the management of the Electric Park seeking new ways to bring customers to the park.

During the early days of the Depression, several amusement parks in the area were forced to close. The Rainbow Electric Park soon felt the sting of the hard times and was forced to close its doors. Over the next few years, the park with its attractions slowly disappeared. This once proud amusement park was all but forgotten during the years of the Great Depression, when the local economy all but came to a standstill. While many people throughout the United States had to leave home looking for work and a way to survive, the great amusement parks and lakes and the wonderful times here were forgotten.

On a day that would live in infamy, December 7, 1941, many Americans felt the pain of being plunged into war. These young men and women had to grow up all too quickly and leave home to work in the war effort. Teenagers took jobs in factories and industries making war materials or bearing arms on foreign soil to defend their homes and families. Many of these young men recalled places such as the Electric Park, and they would long for the hot summer days spent there. Many of them would never return to the Gadsden and Etowah County area.

The year 1945 saw the latest "war to end all wars" coming to a close. As many young men returned to Gadsden, they were disappointed to find that very little remained of the Electric Park. Practically everything was gone of this once popular park. The dance pavilion and the shooting gallery were gone. The skating rink and the bowling lanes had also been torn down. Very little remained of the swimming pool except for the pool's sides, and the entire area was overgrown with thorn bushes. The area was used as a dumping site. During this time, the amusement park was slowly forgotten.

Legend has it that on warm spring and hot summer nights, the spirits of many of the people who never returned from World War II return to this site to enjoy the amusements of the park. Another legend says that spirits from the small cemetery that was located nearby come down to the park. These voices supposedly sound much like a crowd of happy carnival patrons. Whatever the explanation for this legend, many people avoid this area after nightfall. This is a legend that is almost too fantastic to be true. This once popular amusement park has all but faded into Etowah County's haunted past.

Part III

Mysteries of Alabama City

Alabama City was founded as an industrial area between Gadsden and Attalla. Captain James M. Elliott Jr. had become a resident of Gadsden and opened several major businesses in the area. With the help of his father-in-law, Colonel R.B. Kyle, Elliott began to draw up plans for a new town about two miles west of Gadsden. Elliott's dream was to develop this new town as an industrial center and, eventually, merge this town with Gadsden and Attalla into one major city. The town became a reality in 1890 when Elliott, Kyle and T.S. Kyle met to found the town of Alabama City.

At the time of the founding, Alabama City was a very sparsely settled area, not the large industrial development Elliott had envisioned. The town grew slowly at first, although early the following year Elliott filed for incorporation, and a charter was granted in 1891.

Elliott applied for a post office for the new village in 1891. A post office was granted, and Elliott directed the mail from the car works through the Alabama City Post Office to pay the first postmaster, J.K. Fleming. This large volume of mail gave the new post office a substantial amount of business during its early days. The first elections were held in March 1891, with William Gardner elected the town's first mayor.

Elliott and R.B. Kyle worked tirelessly to bring a major industry to the Alabama City area for the next few years. This effort was rewarded in 1895 when an announcement was made by the Dwight Manufacturing Company of Chicopee, Massachusetts, that a large cotton mill would be located in the town. The company sent officials to the three-thousand-acre town to begin plans to bring the industry to Etowah County. Kyle offered to donate the land to build the textile plant. The mill was opened in 1896.

With the effects of the Great Depression lingering and Alabama City unable to meet its payroll, the only solution appeared to be a merger with Gadsden. The vote came about July 12, 1932. Mayor R.D. Morgan thought that the merger with Gadsden would help relieve the financial crunch. The citizens of Alabama City voted 520 to 153 in favor of merging with Gadsden. Alabama City officially became part of the city of Gadsden on July 13, 1932.

Since the 1890s, Alabama City has had its share of tragedies, ghost stories and haunted buildings and things that could never be explained. These events even include a story of a haunted school that had its beginnings in the days of the Civil War way back in 1863. Other ghost stories include a circus tragedy and a streetcar accident that may have caused several eerie sights and sounds since the tragedies. Another strange story that has grown from this area of Gadsden tells of a haunted cemetery where the unmarked, sunken graves have produced ghostly sightings.

A Prediction of Destruction

A woman residing on the western outskirts of Gadsden during the early 1900s attracted a great deal of attention in this area by her dire and dreadful prophesies—many of which turned out to be true. One prediction made in June 1903 caused a mild panic in Etowah County. She said that Alabama City would be destroyed on July 4, 1903, in a fierce tornado. Just why anybody ever thought she knew such things or even dreamed of them was not known. She also claimed that she frequently foretold events.

Although most people claimed not to believe in the predictions, this prophecy caused many residents of Gadsden, Alabama City and Attalla to become very frightened. The woman predicted that early in the morning of July 4, a terrific tornado would strike the mill village and would sweep away everything before it. She said that the large cotton mill of the Dwight Manufacturing Company would be totally destroyed and that many of its operatives would be killed or injured. The aged woman had a vivid imagination, and she went into detail about the damage to be done by the great storm. She also said that the furnaces and steel mill under construction nearby would also be blown away.

Downtown Alabama City showing Wall Street. This city was predicted to be destroyed in a tornado, but that never happened.

At the time of this scare, the Dwight Manufacturing Company was operating at an all-time high. The prediction of the giant cotton mill's destruction actually caused some of its employees to quit their jobs and move out of Etowah County. Some believed that the large mill village's destruction would be caused by the wickedness of its people, although Alabama City was a very quiet place and the rate of crime there was the lowest of any city in Etowah County. The fear of this impending doom seemed to overshadow the plans of the upcoming Independence Day.

As the days slowly rolled around to the Fourth of July, holiday plans were made. Picnics and cookouts were planned throughout the county, although many people were still keeping a close watch on the weather. On the day before the holiday, some people sent their families to visit relatives just in case. On July 4, people here awoke to a beautiful summer morning. Picnics, baseball games, fishing and swimming went on as planned. The millworkers were enjoying this special holiday much the same as in years past, although some were still thinking about what the afternoon and evening might hold. They were in hourly dread of the coming disastrous storm. The fact that there was not a cloud in the sky did not ease the fear of what the evening might bring.

As the afternoon slowly progressed, many came out to enjoy the cool water of the huge lake at the back of the mill, as well as a relaxing band concert in the early evening. Many people were still expecting the worst when the bell at the mill tolled the 9:00 p.m. curfew.

When the bell rang again early the next morning to awaken the mill village, it was obvious that this prediction of doom had not come true. The talk at work that morning was of the prediction and the fact that nothing had come about. Most everyone said that they didn't believe the prediction, and things slowly began to get back to normal at the cotton mill.

THE HAUNTED SCHOOL

Everyone who has lived in the Etowah County area for a very long time has no doubt heard the story of Emma Sansom. This story has been told and retold for more than 140 years. The story has grown into a local legend that has added much to the history of Etowah County. While many of the details of this story are well known, there are a few that are not quite so well remembered.

The incident at Black Creek happened on a warm spring morning in 1863. Colonel Abel Streight and a large number of Union cavalry were passing through the Gadsden area en route to Rome, Georgia, to capture this important city. Streight was being hindered in his quest by Confederate cavalry leader Nathan Bedford Forrest. While Streight's orders were to plunder and burn everything in his path, Forrest was following close enough to disrupt his plans. When Streight reached the bridge across Black Creek just west of Gadsden, Forrest was only about two hours behind. To slow Forrest's pursuit, Streight ordered the bridge across the rain-swollen creek burned, and snipers were also positioned near the creek.

When Forrest arrived a short time later, the bridge was completely engulfed in flames. Emma Sansom, who lived near the present site of the school that bears her name, volunteered to show the Confederate leader another place to cross the creek. During the crossing, Robert Turner was killed by a Union sniper's bullet. He was buried in the Sansom cemetery near the family home. Forrest pursued Streight, overtook him near Cedar Bluff, Alabama, and tricked him into surrendering. Streight, with a much larger force, surrendered to Forrest and was marched into Rome in much humiliation.

The 1935 graduating class of Emma Sansom High School is shown here outside the school building. This structure was reported as being haunted by many over the years.

The facts of the story are accurate. Few people are aware, however, that General Forrest returned to the Etowah County area a few days later. Forrest first came to visit his friend R.B. Kyle. Forrest stayed at the Kyle home, which was located at the present site of the Etowah County Courthouse. This beautiful home would later be the residence of Captain James M. Elliott Jr. General Forrest spent the night sleeping in a bed for the first time in weeks. The following morning, Colonel R.B. Kyle treated Forrest to a breakfast of hotcakes and sausages. The general spent the remainder of the morning playing with the Kyle children.

At about noon, Forrest mounted his horse to leave to rejoin his troops. T.S. Kyle cried for Forrest to take him for a ride on his horse. Forrest lifted the two-year-old into the saddle with him and rode off in the direction of Attalla. Colonel Kyle followed to bring T.S. Kyle back home after about a mile or so.

Forrest made one other stop in the Gadsden area. The Confederate leader paid a visit to the Sansom home to convey his thanks to the young girl who had exhibited such bravery several days earlier. After this short visit, Forrest rode off toward Guntersville and into history. Emma Sansom was rewarded for her act of courage. An award of land was given to her by a grateful

The haunted school as it appears today in an abandoned state.

State of Alabama. This gift was short-lived, however, when the Confederacy surrendered in 1865. The award that was given to Emma Sansom was taken away when Alabama was readmitted to the Union.

In 1929, Alabama City built a new high school and named it in honor of Emma Sansom. This beautiful school was built on the banks of Black Creek near the location of the incident of 1863. The strange happenings at this beautiful school building began almost immediately. Odd sounds could be heard in the original portion of this school, which had been enlarged several times since its construction. These sounds were almost like muffled voices and loud noises, similar to a fight or skirmish taking place on the banks of the creek. These events usually happened when there were very few people around. There was also one particular room in the school that would give the effect of it spinning at times. This sensation was never explained.

Possible explanations of these sounds and voices were usually dismissed as the sounds of an old building that was near seventy-five years old when it was closed with the building of the new Gadsden City High School. In recent years, the building suffered a destructive fire, and much of the old structure was torn away. Did Robert Turner return to the area where he was killed in the War Between the States?

The Ghost at Station No. 4

For more than one hundred years, Etowah County has attempted to provide the finest in fire protection. Several fire stations are located throughout the many municipalities in the county. Gadsden has had the finest equipment that could be offered since the late nineteenth century, including the first paid department and the first motorized fire engines in Etowah County. Firefighting in Alabama City was handled a little differently in the early years of the twentieth century. When the Dwight Manufacturing Company put a giant textile plant in the small town, plans were made for adequate fire protection.

A huge lake was located at the rear of the cotton mill that was fed by an underground spring. Water was pumped from Black Creek, as well as from the lake to a large reservoir on a hill overlooking the mill village. Water from this reservoir was used to fight fires throughout the village.

An extensive fire hydrant system was installed in the village. The cotton mill had a large firefighting department, and hundreds of feet of fire hose were stored in small buildings around the mill. Wagons transported the hose to the scene if a fire broke out in the residential or business district of Alabama City.

The old Gadsden Fire Station No. 4 in Alabama City. Several reports surfaced of a ghost that haunted the upstairs bedroom area.

On February 6, 1929, action by the Alabama City Council began to change this. On February 7, the council officially accepted a new motorized fire engine built by the American-LaFrance Company at a cost of $12,500.

The machine was a combination pump, hose and booster tank truck that was specially built for use by small cities and was regarded as one of the best and most effective made. It was the first real firefighting apparatus that the big mill town had ever owned. Before this purchase, the mill village had depended on a homemade hose truck that had given good service but that was entirely dependent on gravity pressure.

The new machine had been put through its final paces the day before in a three-hour pumping test at the lake at the Dwight Manufacturing Company. It was said to live up to all of the claims made for it by the manufacturers. This new firefighting apparatus would be a welcome addition if a major fire broke out in either Gadsden or Attalla.

In addition to approving the purchase of the new fire truck, the council also adopted a new plumbing ordinance that was somewhat similar to the one in operation in Gadsden. This was made necessary, officials said, by the building boom going on in Alabama City as a result of the industrial explosion in Gadsden.

Plans were originally announced on March 1, 1938, to build a new fire station in the Alabama City area of Gadsden. The original plans called for work on the new station to begin on March 15, with original construction costs to be about $18,000. Work actually began on April 18 due to bad weather. Work would finally be completed the following year, with a formal dedication planned for March 7, 1939. The proposal to dedicate the fine new fire station was suggested by the Civitan Club of Alabama City. Plans were also made by the Civitans to sponsor a silver tea on the same day in order to raise money for purchasing kitchen equipment for the station.

The Civitans took up the matter of dedicating the building since most residents in the Alabama City area took particular pride in the new station. The new fire station was considered by many to be a model one in this part of Alabama. The Civitans also took an active role in raising money for items for the kitchen. The firemen had been attempting to secure a lot of secondhand equipment at their own expense. The plan to dedicate the station was presented to the city commission, which readily and unanimously agreed to participate.

A large crowd of more than seven hundred was on hand to inspect the new Alabama City Fire Station during an open house that took place before the dedication on March 7, 1939. The formal dedication took place at 3:15

p.m. The tea, sponsored by the Alabama City Civitan Club, brought in a substantial amount of money to help furnish the kitchen for the new station. The tea was free, with donations being accepted. These proceeds were also used to help equip the living quarters of the new station.

The Emma Sansom High School band, under the direction of Mort Glosser, entertained the large crowd before the formal dedication ceremony began. Reverend Zack Appleton, a member of the Civitan Club committee in charge of the club's part of the celebration, opened the formal proceedings with an invocation and presided as master of ceremonies. Other speakers included A.F. Leavitt and A.L. Morton.

Chairman J.H. Meighan, of the Gadsden City Commission, was present and gave the principal address of the day. After complimenting the Civitan Club for its work in the interest of the community, he stated that he did not believe that a finer building of its kind existed in the state of Alabama. Mr. Meighan pointed out that this modern, two-story structure had been erected at very little cost to the city. He stated that the city spent only $4,778.72 of its money to get the building, which cost a total of $25,627.24. At the time of the opening of this new station, the Gadsden Fire Department had a total of thirty-two firemen. Associate Commissioner Gordon Cantrell and Fire Chief S.T. Green were present but did not speak.

Soon after the fire station was opened, the strange noises began. Unusual sounds could be heard in the downstairs restroom, and at times the toilet would flush without anyone being there. The firemen, who worked twenty-four hours and were off forty-eight, would always check to see if anyone was there. This usually turned up nothing. For a while, these sounds were nerve-wracking, although they eventually were just accepted as the ghost in the engine room. As quickly as these sounds were accepted, a new sighting began to take place.

The "ghost" began to take a different form and moved to the sleeping quarters. The first sighting happened late at night, when a dark figure was seen walking from bed to bed. When the lights were turned on, the figure vanished. This went on for many months, and soon this ghostly figure was accepted as simply the "ghost at Number 4."

Eventually a new fire station was built in the Alabama City area of Gadsden. Today this structure houses the Alabama City Historical Association. It is being restored and turned into a museum. This museum will house exhibits from the early days of the area that was once known as Alabama City. The strange sounds and reported sightings of the ghostly specter remain until this day.

HAUNTED POTTER'S FIELD

Many towns throughout the United States have a cemetery that is said to be haunted. These graveyards are thought to be visited by the spirits of the dearly departed that cannot find rest for one reason or another. These cemeteries usually have strange sights and sounds that are experienced after nightfall. For many years now, a small cemetery in Alabama City has had the distinction of being haunted by several unidentified people who are buried here. These graves are close to one hundred years old and date back to the influenza pandemic of 1918. These poor, unfortunate victims were buried in this potter's field that was designated for homeless victims of this great epidemic.

An article appeared in the October 3, 1918 *Gadsden Daily Times-News* concerning a recent outbreak of influenza or flu. Dr. E.T. Camp, Etowah County medical officer, said that several cases of "grippe" (another term for the flu) were reported in the city but that these probably were just the plain old American disease that was reported each year. There was a fear, though, that the Spanish flu germ had reached the city, and precautions were necessary at that time.

In the fall of 1918, the Great War in Europe was winding down, and peace was on the horizon. The Americans had joined in the fight, bringing the Allies closer to victory against the Germans. Deep within the trenches, these men lived through some of the most brutal conditions of life.

Then, in pockets across the globe, something erupted that seemed as benign as the common cold at first. The influenza of that season, however, was far worse. In two years, one-fifth of the world's population was infected. The flu was deadliest for people twenty to forty years old. An estimated 675,000 Americans died of influenza during the pandemic, ten times as many as in the world war. Of the U.S. soldiers who died in Europe, half of them fell to the influenza virus and not to the enemy. An estimated 43,000 servicemen mobilized for World War I died of influenza. The year 1918 was unforgettable as a year of suffering and death—and yet also of peace.

With more cases of the grippe being reported each day, an emergency meeting of the Gadsden City Council was called. Dr. C.L. Murphree, Gadsden health officer, and Camp each advised the council not to panic. Amid protests by Judge J.H. Disque, the city council voted to close all schools, both public and private. Gadsden mayor W.P. Johnson issued a proclamation on October 9, 1918, closing schools, theaters, lodges, poolrooms and all

It is almost impossible to get to the potter's field in Alabama City because of the underbrush.

places of public meetings until further notice. For the first time in the history of the city of Gadsden, all churches and Sunday schools were ordered closed until further notice.

By October 15, 1918, 908 cases had been reported, although only 4 deaths had been reported. These numbers were not very accurate, however, because not all doctors in the county reported to the county health officer. The following day, the number of reported cases of Spanish influenza had grown to 1,642. By day three, there were 2,090 cases reported throughout the county. Murphree was confident on this date, however, that the number of cases would begin to drop, although the number of fatalities would begin to rise. He expressed optimism the epidemic would pass within two weeks. Another 280 cases were reported the next day, bringing the total to 2,370. Places of assembly remained closed throughout much of October. The ban was lifted on October 30, 1918. Schools were opened the following Monday, with churches resuming services immediately. Movie theaters were the only exception. Camp asked anyone who was infected to stay away from these meeting places.

With one-quarter of the U.S. and one-fifth of the world infected with influenza, it was impossible to escape from the illness. Even President

Woodrow Wilson suffered from the flu in early 1919 while negotiating the crucial Treaty of Versailles to end the First World War. Accurate records of reported cases and deaths in Etowah County will probably never be known. There is a small cemetery in Alabama City with several unmarked graves reportedly holding the remains of victims from the flu epidemic of 1918.

This small cemetery was soon forgotten because of the unmarked graves and the unkempt condition of the graveyard. As the decades passed, the graves slowly sank in, and the local residents soon forgot the cemetery until the first strange things were heard and the unexplained lights were seen in this wooded area just off Marston Avenue in Alabama City. Many teenagers who had heard the legend of this haunted cemetery would make the short walk to this area to attempt to frighten their friends. At first the cemetery was just an eerie party place until people began to hear the strange sounds and voices once again.

Local legend has it that the spirits of the victims of this great influenza epidemic of 1918 are still walking this desolate wooded area on certain nights. Are the eerie lights that have been reported from time to time and the voices that have been heard only hoaxes meant to scare people who have been taken to this area after sundown, or are they real and this area actually haunted by ghosts of a forgotten era?

THE HAUNTED CIRCUS GROUNDS

For the people living in Alabama City during the early 1900s, work hours were long and hard. Working at the steel plant and the cotton mill was tough, and the workweek was usually six days long. Times to rest and relax were eagerly anticipated, and ballgames, street fairs and the arrival of the circus were major events. For several weeks, the coming of the Christy Brothers Circus was widely publicized throughout Etowah County. When the day of the show's arrival came, plans were underway to dismiss schools early to allow everyone to come to the circus parade.

The circus arrived in the early hours of the morning and set up on the grounds near the present site of Emma Sansom Middle School. Plans were for a grand parade from the circus grounds to Wall Street and back. The circus was to put on its first show that afternoon and another that evening.

The old field where a circus tragedy took place that claimed the lives of several circus animals and two innocent bystanders.

The circus would be in Alabama City for several days, giving everyone in Etowah County a chance to see the show.

On the morning of the parade, a crowd of curious onlookers was gathering at the circus grounds on Kyle Avenue. The parade was to begin at 10:00 a.m., although a thunderstorm appeared in the distance. Because of this apparent storm, the local schools decided to delay closing, although this meant that many children would miss the parade and the first performance of the circus. As the skies began to turn darker, cloud-to-ground lightning was witnessed coming closer and closer. Before the crowd could disperse and take shelter, tragedy unfolded.

A bolt of lightning struck an overhead high-voltage power line and cross arm near the crowd assembled to watch the parade. The power line burned with a bright flame and then fell into the crowd. The electric wire carried twenty-two thousand volts from the steam plant to the car barn and then to Attalla. When this power line hit the ground, everyone nearby was knocked off his or her feet. Several large, beautiful white circus horses were killed, with nine others being killed ten minutes later in a second blinding flash. Speculation as to the cause of this second flash was that the current was turned back on while the wire was on the wet ground. Fifteen circus horses were killed in this mishap.

Thomas Bowling, an electric company employee, was on hand as the events of the morning unfolded. When the high-voltage line fell, he contacted the steam plant and had the power turned off. He then prepared to cut the power line. As Bowling began to cut the wire, the power evidently was turned back on, killing Bowling instantly. Another bystander, Imogene Isaacs of Alabama City, was also killed in this mishap. Five others were seriously injured and were rushed to the Ralls Sanatorium, while many were treated at the scene for a variety of injuries.

The circus tragedy of Alabama City was the talk of the entire county. News quickly spread of the events of this day. Grief-stricken residents of the small mill village hurried to the schools to see if their children were okay. Since the schools had not dismissed earlier in the day, a major loss of life had been averted thanks to the Alabama City Board of Education.

The burial and disposal of the dead animals took several days. The strange sounds and sightings at the circus grounds began almost immediately. A sound similar to thunder was reported at times, and a bright blinding flash could be seen and heard on occasion. Although the sounds of this tragic day vanished when Gulf Steel School was built on the site in the 1950s, strange noises could at times be heard in the school building itself. Today these frightening noises are nonexistent since the new school has been built here. Whatever the explanation, this story has slowly faded into the history of Alabama City and Gadsden.

A GHOSTLY RIVALRY

From the early days of the twentieth century, there have been many amusement parks located throughout the Etowah County area. Although many of these lakes and amusement parks have proven to be very popular, none of them seems to have survived the changing of time. While these places were locally famous, probably the most popular early amusement park in Etowah County was Elliott Lake Park, later known as the Masonic Lake. Although this area was a great place to have fun, the location of this lake is all but forgotten.

Elliott Lake Park was an important amusement park that was opened during the latter part of 1908. The park came about following the opening of the steel plant. The park was meant to offer a recreational facility to the many workers at the steel plant and the hundreds of laborers at the Dwight Mill. The lake was built by the Schuler brothers, who brought the steel plant here, and was named after Captain James Elliott, one of the founders of Alabama City.

Elliott Lake was an instant success. When the lake was first opened, there was canoeing and fishing, a dance pavilion, an athletic field for baseball and football and an open-air theater. During the early years of the park, Elliott Lake was the home of the Gadsden Steelmakers, a minor-league baseball team. This athletic field was also the home of many early football games, as well as the first high school football games played by Etowah and Disque High Schools.

Later, several amusement rides were added to the park, as well as a large concrete-lined swimming pool. The swimming pool had a large well house that pumped fresh water to the pool, which was from two feet deep in the shallow end to nine feet in the deep end. A concession stand was located next to the well house. There were men's and ladies' bathhouses located at each

The 1910 Etowah County football squad met Disque High School on the gridiron several times at Elliott Lake Park.

end of the swimming pool. The large skating rink that was originally located at the lake was built as an open-air rink but was later glassed in so it could be used year round. The great orator William Jennings Bryan made a public speaking appearance here.

The lake also had a theater that showed many popular movies over the years. The electric streetcars would make special runs when a movie was showing to return movie patrons to Gadsden and Attalla. During the warm summer months, many band concerts were featured at the lake's large bandstand. Again the streetcars would run into the night to carry the many concertgoers home.

The lake would later be purchased by the local Masonic lodge and become known as the Masonic Lake. A member of the Masonic lodge could go to the lake for an afternoon of swimming and not have to pay. A nonmember of the lodge could go with a member and pay fifteen to twenty-five cents to swim. The lake remained a popular amusement area until the Depression years of 1929 and 1930, when the pool was closed.

In searching for the area that contained Elliott Lake Park, later known as the Masonic Lake, one would drive west on Meighan Boulevard, which was called Elliott Avenue. One would then turn right on Shaddix Street and go past the home of Dr. Shaddix. A person would cross the old Southern Railroad tracks and through a large gate to enter the park. After entering this large fenced area, one would proceed to the parking area and the concession stands and pump houses.

The bathhouses were next, with a large, 30-foot by 60-foot swimming pool located between. Moving on west to Attalla was Elliott Lake, which was used for fishing and canoeing. This lake was about 450 feet long and 60 feet wide. Farther west was the old athletic fields and band box.

The first local high school to field a football team was Disque High School in 1909. The Disque team began practice in mid-September, preparing for the season opener on October 9, 1909. The first team was coached in its early days by Kyle Elliott. The team was expected to be competitive, although its first game was an extremely tough one against a much larger squad from the Agricultural College of the Seventh Congressional District of Albertville.

The Disque team took the train to Albertville on the morning of the game and met the favored Albertville squad. The Disque team was outweighed forty pounds to the man and was defeated soundly by the home team, 36–0. The Albertville team scored five touchdowns in the first half and kicked one goal. In the second half, Disque held Albertville to one touchdown. At that time, a touchdown was 5 points and a goal kicked was 1 point.

Two weeks later, the Disque team met Bessemer High School in its first home game of the 1909 football season. The streetcars brought several hundred fans to Elliott Lake to see this memorable high school contest. Disque quickly took control of the game, scoring twice in the first half and twice in the second. Two goals were kicked, and Disque brought home its first win by a final score of 22–0.

The following year, Etowah High School fielded its first football team. Disque High School and Etowah High met twice during the 1910 football season, with Disque winning both contests. This was the beginning of an intense rivalry that continued for many years. When the new Gadsden High School was built and Disque became a junior high school, the Disque-Etowah rivalry would carry over as the Gadsden-Etowah rivalry.

Legend has it that these first teams from Disque and Etowah High School meet twice a year each fall to continue this once great rivalry. These two proud football powers are located less than five miles apart, and it was probably the most hotly contested rivalry in north Alabama. On these days each fall, this overgrown area is the site of two ghostly teams battling for Etowah County football supremacy.

PART IV
ATTALLA

The city of Attalla is the second-largest city in Etowah County. This town from its early beginnings has had a very colorful and exciting history. Attalla was incorporated on February 5, 1872, after being founded in 1870.

Attalla has had a very colorful history as both a quiet mining community and a bustling railroad center of Etowah County. Attalla was also the original home of the Alabama Power Company. Captain William P. Lay founded Alabama Power Company in 1906 in Gadsden along with his son, Earl. Attorney O.R. Hood, had started building a hydro-generating plant at the old Wesson Mill on Big Wills Creek in 1902 that later supplied power to the city of Attalla.

Since the 1870s, the city of Attalla has adapted to the changing economy. The railroads that were so important to the city's economy experienced times of bankruptcy, and the town's financial leaders turned to the area's natural resources for help. Large deposits of coal and iron ore were mined in the mountains surrounding the town, bringing jobs to Attalla. In the late 1880s, Attalla was noted as being the largest iron ore shipping point in the state.

Attalla has had its share of ghosts and unexplainable sightings over the years. Some of these were associated with the railroads and the local saloons. Another eerie story is associated with one of Etowah County's "haunted bridges."

THE HAUNTED SALOON

Over the years, many of the older buildings in downtown Attalla have been rumored to be haunted. These unusual occurrences are often unexplained noises or things that mysteriously move or seem to vanish. Many times these are caused by a tragic event that took place there. One such event took place at a downtown Attalla saloon during the early twentieth century.

This is the case of Attalla police chief Pink Jenkins and the sacrifice he made on September 26, 1903. On this Saturday evening, Chief Jenkins would lose his life at one of the saloons located in downtown Attalla. During the early 1900s, there were several saloons located in downtown Gadsden and Attalla. These businesses were popular places, although the incidences of violence were growing at an alarming rate. This violence would continue until many people began to cry out for the closing of the open saloon in Etowah County.

Fowler's Saloon was one of the popular saloons located on Fifth Avenue in downtown Attalla. This saloon, much like the others located here, attracted a rough crowd, and the local police departments had to answer many calls there during the weekends. Most of the customers of these saloons were usually heavily armed, and many stabbings and shootings occurred here.

Pink Jenkins was a popular Attalla police officer who was elected as an extra policeman by the Attalla City Council in early 1903. He was considered a fearless police officer and was respected by many of the citizens of Attalla. He shot and killed a suspect he was attempting to take into custody at the Union Passenger Station in March 1903. Most of the citizens of Attalla sided with the popular officer, and within six months he was serving the Attalla Police Department as chief of police. On September 26, 1903, Chief Jenkins would meet his destiny as bravely as he had fulfilled his duty as an Attalla policeman.

On this Saturday night, Chief Jenkins was making his rounds in downtown Attalla. He was walking into Fowler's Saloon when the sound of a gunshot caused Jenkins to go to the rear of the saloon to look into it. Upon further investigation, Chief Jenkins found two men shooting at an elderly man. Jenkins went to one of the men, took hold of him and told him that he must come with him. As Jenkins took hold of the suspect, the other man interfered, and the three men began to struggle. Two eyewitnesses to the struggle said that one of the suspects pointed his gun at the officer and opened fire.

After the shooting in the rear of the saloon, the two men ran out the back door. Near the bell tower, they met Attalla policeman Blankenship, who called to them to halt, but instead they opened fire on Blankenship, striking him in the left shoulder. Blankenship returned fire, striking one suspect in the left arm, and then turned and exchanged shots with the other until his gun was empty.

After the shooting, officer Blankenship returned to the saloon to check on the condition of his chief. A physician was summoned to attend to Chief Jenkins, and after making his examination, Dr. Wilson reported that Jenkins would not live much longer. Chief Jenkins died about fifteen minutes later.

The two suspects were later identified as John White and his brother-in-law, Charles Gibbs. After the shooting, White went to the home of Dr. Stewart to have the bullet wound in his left arm dressed. White returned with Dr. Stewart to his office, at which time he was taken into custody for the killing of the Attalla police chief.

Charley Gibbs fled the city, and a reward was placed on his head as an accomplice to the murder of Jenkins. John White and Charley Gibbs had moved to Attalla two years earlier from Rockwood, Tennessee, to work in the mines of the North Alabama Mining Company.

The funeral for Police Chief Pink Jenkins was held at the Methodist Church of Attalla on Monday, September 28, 1903. The police departments of Gadsden and Alabama City turned out in large numbers to pay their last respects to this popular police officer. Jenkins was remembered as a fearless officer who enforced the law without favor.

Soon after the tragedy at Fowler's Saloon, strange and unexplainable events began to take place. Odd sounds very similar to gunshots could be heard at the rear of the building. At times voices could be heard in the saloon, but upon investigation no one was found in the building. A few short years later, Etowah County was voted dry, and the saloons in downtown Attalla were closed. The voices and strange sounds associated with this building and the tragic event that took place here were soon forgotten. Legend has it that this dedicated police officer still walks his beat in downtown Attalla.

The Haunted Railroad

Attalla, Alabama, has the distinction of being the second-largest city in Etowah County. While the town is smaller in area and population than Gadsden, the city has a rich history. When the small town of Attalla was founded, plans were put into motion to create an industrial and transportation

The railroad yard in Attalla was a busy place, with the many trains arriving and departing each day. Several accidents have taken place here over the years.

center in Etowah County. Several railroad lines passed through Etowah County at this point, and a city soon began to grow here. This new town located near Gadsden would soon develop into a small city, and plans were made to seek incorporation. The United States government was petitioned for a post office, and the name of "Newton" was chosen, although Alabama already had a city named this. The name of Attalla was later chosen, and the junction of the railroads would become known as Attalla.

Through the years, there have been many discussions on how the town got this name, as well as its exact meaning. One theory is that the first Indian settlement here was known as Atale, which is a form of the Cherokee word *Otali*, which means "mountain." Another theory is that this word probably means "my home," and this is accepted by most authorities.

Attalla began to thrive and grow in 1870 when Stanton, Cravath and Stanton completed its Wills Valley Railroad from Chattanooga along Lookout Mountain to its southernmost point, where Attalla is now. The company built a large hotel and began to lay out a town, which was called Newton in honor of the old hometown. Several other railroads merged here, making Newton an important junction for such transportation. A grand hotel was built to serve as a depot and restaurant. This hotel was a replica of the Stanton House in Chattanooga and was famous for its great food. One of Attalla's early landmarks, it burned down several years later.

Through the years, the city of Attalla has adapted to the changing economy. The railroads that were so important to the city's economy experienced times of bankruptcy, and the town's financial leaders turned to the area's natural resources for help. Large deposits of coal and iron ore were mined in the mountains surrounding the town, bringing jobs. In the late 1880s, Attalla was noted as being the largest iron ore shipping point in the state.

The different railroads brought many people to the Etowah County area. Dignitaries and travelers all passed through the Attalla railroad terminal and stayed at the grand hotel. While the railroads brought much commerce to the area, they also brought stories of ghosts and haunted hotels. Several tragic accidents associated with the railroads helped to fuel the fire about the railway being haunted.

During the days of the Great Depression, many people had to take to the road in search of work. Many transients would stow away in railroad cars and ride the rails from town to town, searching for food and work. Although many people would hop a freight and sleep in the rail yards, this was a very dangerous practice. Several accidental deaths took place in the rail yard in Attalla and on the tracks leading to Attalla.

The beautiful hotel that was once located near the passenger terminal was reported to be haunted on many occasions. One room was the scene of a death many years ago, and guests given that particular room always reported a strange presence there and would always ask to have their accommodations changed. These strange happenings disappeared after the hotel burned down.

For more than a century, many ghost stories have been told about the freight yard and the strange sightings here. Strange lights have been seen here, and people have been reported walking the rails just south of the city. The railroads have slowly been phased out in the Etowah County area with the coming of improved roads. Passenger train service no longer goes through Attalla, and the freight trains make fewer stops here each day. The rail stations have been gone now for many years, and the grand hotel burned down decades ago. Today, little remains of the legends and ghost stories that have been told and retold here for many years.

Attalla's Haunted Bridge

Almost every town in the United States has a haunted bridge. These bridges have been favorite scenes for ghost stories, murders, tragic accidents and haunting stories for more than one hundred years. Usually these bridges are made of wood and/or steel and seem to make ghostly sounds as automobile traffic passes over them. Gruesome stories have been gradually embellished to go with these old structures. Etowah County has the honor of having two such structures. One of the county's haunted bridges is located on the old Boaz Road in Attalla near the downtown business district.

Legend has it that a school bus ran off this bridge in the early days of the twentieth century, with several fatalities. For many years, strange things have been reported on and around this old structure. At times passersby could hear the horrifying sounds of the bus crash and the cries of the unfortunate students who were on this old bus. Another story that is told about this haunted bridge is that if a vehicle pulls up to the bridge, stops with its front tires on the bridge and puts the car or truck in neutral, the spirits of these children will push the auto across the bridge.

The haunted bridge is located in Attalla on the Old Boaz Road. This is a very spooky site.

Since the 1950s, this old bridge has been a favorite place to try to frighten dates late at night. The old iron and wooden bridge always made eerie sounds as automobiles passed over it. The old secluded road that has long since been replaced as a major road to Marshall County soon became a popular place for beer parties, as well as a parking area.

Today, Attalla's haunted bridge has been abandoned and is no longer useable. This old structure, complete with its ghosts and eerie past, stands alone and all but forgotten. The story of a tragic bus crash has never been substantiated. All that remains is a desolate structure and the legend that has entertained Etowah County residents for decades.

Part V
Etowah County Ghosts

Etowah County has a rich and colorful history. Many interesting and unusual stories have been told from the early days of Baine County and, later, Etowah County, which has had an abundance of monsters and ghosts that have been reported and discussed for more than 145 years. These sightings have been reported not only in the larger cities but also in the less populated areas in the county. These stories include Indian legends, as well as a creature that terrorized Gallant for sometime and ghosts in the Happy Hill and Crudup communities. Etowah County has also had several UFOs reported since the end of World War II from several prominent citizens.

While many of these stories are probably the products of an overactive imagination, old county legends or an actual sighting of a paranormal occurrence, they have been reported for many years.

Crudup's Haunted Hotel

The town of Crudup had its beginnings in 1880 when the Crudup Mining Company of Chattooga, Georgia, struck a rich vein of iron ore on Lookout Ridge. With the opening of the mine, a railroad spur to the Great Southern Railroad had to be built. A town quickly grew around

Crudup was a thriving mining community in the late 1800s and early 1900s. The mines eventually dried up, and the area is a ghost town today.

the railroad, with a hotel, a post office, several stores and many small homes. As the town grew, so did the need for adequate police protection, prompting the Etowah County Sheriff's Department to station a deputy in the town. One of those deputies became the first Etowah County deputy sheriff to lose his life.

Ernest W. Birt was a special deputy sheriff serving in the Crudup area. He was a seasoned officer, having served as Attalla's chief of police before joining the sheriff's department. He left the Attalla Police Department after a prisoner in his custody was killed resisting arrest. Birt moved on to the job of patrolling the area around Crudup. He met his date with destiny following a domestic dispute with a young miner.

Birt was making his rounds around the mines at about 10:00 a.m. on February 14, 1911. He was walking past the hotel and the commissary when someone stepped out of the barbershop, pointed a pistol at the back of Birt's head and fired. Birt slumped to the ground as his assailant fled

Very few of the buildings remain at Crudup. Many have burned down or have been torn down.

toward Attalla. Birt was taken to the office of Dr. Cramp, who said that the wounded officer would not live.

At 11:00 a.m., a phone call was placed to Etowah County sheriff Lister about the shooting. Lister and Deputy Farrar left immediately for the crime scene. Dr. Cramp pronounced Birt dead at 1:10 p.m.

Bob Styles, a twenty-three-year old miner, was arrested shortly after the shooting by Deputy Painter, who also was stationed at Crudup. Painter had been summoned shortly after the shooting. He met Styles, who confessed to the crime and surrendered. Styles was a resident of a boardinghouse owned by Mrs. Tucker, Birt's mother. Styles and Birt had quarreled more than once about a younger half-sister of Birt's with whom Styles had become involved. Birt had ordered Styles to leave Crudup the morning of the shooting. Styles refused to leave and waited for Birt to make his rounds when the shooting occurred.

Birt was buried at Bethany Cemetery near Reese Station at 2:00 p.m. the following day. He left behind a widow and several children. Styles stood trial for the murder in Etowah County Circuit Court. Birt's shooting caused quite an air of excitement in Crudup. Many of the residents were up in arms over the event, although cooler heads prevailed and the law was allowed to take its course.

Over the next few years, the iron ore mine at Crudup slowly dried up. The fast-growing community soon began to lose its population as miners left the area for work elsewhere. The post office, stores, hotel and other businesses also slowly began to disappear.

Local legend has it that the hotel at Crudup was haunted. At times, the figure of a man was seen sitting on the porch of the hotel, and sometimes this ghostly image was seen walking the streets of the small mining community. Was this the image of the slain officer walking his assigned beat or the spirit of one of the miners who lost his life in an accident in the Crudup mines?

Today little remains of this once thriving mining town. The buildings are all gone, and the legend of a haunted hotel has slowly faded into the history of Etowah County.

THE CRYBABY BRIDGE

Many local ghost stories have grown from tales of tragedy and urban legends that belong strictly to Etowah County. The stories all have a local flair and are told over and over each Halloween.

One story that has grown into an urban legend takes place on Lookout Mountain just outside the Gadsden city limits. This story is known to many local residents by the name "Crybaby Bridge" or, simply, "the Haunted Bridge." Several stories have been told throughout the years to explain the many strange things that have been heard or seen on and around this small bridge. There are probably as many versions of this story as there have been people coming here to try to see a ghost or hear the cries from the bridge.

The bridge was located on Pleasant Hill Road just outside the city limits of Gadsden. The road runs from Tabor Road to Lay Springs Road. The bridge was a small, one-lane structure made of steel and wood. In the past forty years, it has captured the fascination of most teenagers, who come to the area after dark in hopes of seeing or hearing something unusual.

One story told about the bridge is that someone was lynched in the trees near it during the nineteenth century. The story goes on to tell that when a person drives across the bridge after sundown, he can hear the horrifying cries of the victim as he is being hanged.

Another story told about the bridge is of two young boys who went swimming in the waters of Black Creek. One of the boys was reported to have drowned near the bridge and can be heard after nightfall struggling in the water below.

Probably the most popular story that deals with the bridge has to do with a murder that took place nearby. According to this legend, a young mother and her infant child were murdered and the bodies disposed of in the creek near the bridge. This story also says that if a car travels across the bridge three times, one can hear the baby crying and see the young mother on the creek bank below.

Although these stories have been told for many years, there is little evidence to back up the reports of the tragic deaths during the late 1800s. There are no records of a lynching near the bridge or a drowning in this part of Black Creek. There also is no record of a double slaying in this part of Etowah County during the late nineteenth century or early twentieth century. Although these stories cannot be proven, many

The Crybaby Bridge was located on the mountain past Noccalula Falls. The bridge was replaced several years ago.

people tell of the strange noises that can be heard on and around this eerie bridge.

For many of the people living near the bridge on Pleasant Hill Road, the attention the bridge has gotten has been a nuisance. At times, the flood of people coming to the quiet area has been almost too much to bear. Many people dismiss this ghost story as a hoax that began when someone hung a sheet in a tree and made up a story in an attempt to scare his friends.

To many other people, the strange noises that can be heard are too real to overlook. The strange sounds and sights in this very quiet area of Etowah County make this urban legend or Etowah County ghost story very real.

The bridge was built in 1882, according to local records. It first was installed at Walnut Grove. In the mid-1930s, it was taken apart, moved above the falls and reassembled on Pleasant Hill Road. It is believed to be the oldest surviving bridge in Etowah County. The bridge has had a weight limit for several years preventing school buses, fire trucks and other heavy vehicles from crossing it. The county commission approved a contract with the Alabama Department of Transportation to replace the bridge using money that the county received as part of the statewide program started several years ago to replace bridges that have posted weight limits that cause school bus detours. It is a wrought-iron, Pratt truss bridge. It was built from parts that came from the Bethlehem Iron Company, which later became Bethlehem Steel. The floor I-beams were the first of their kind in America to be rolled and were made by the Trenton Iron Company.

The bridge has been saved and moved to nearby Attalla. The moving of the old Pleasant Hill Road Bridge is the first step toward developing the intersection of Cleveland Avenue and U.S. Highway 431. The question remains as to whether the ghosts and tales of the eerie sights and sounds associated with this bridge will follow the structure to its new home or simply fade into Etowah County's haunted past.

THE HORROR OF HAPPY HILL

During the past one hundred years or more, several unexplained events unfold in the course of history that slowly are forgotten or are lost in the pages of old, yellowed newspapers. One such mystery happened in the small

Happy Hill is located near Sardis. This area of Etowah County once had many government stills located here.

community of Happy Hill near Sardis during the spring of 1875. This event has to do with the unsolved murder of a revenue officer, as well as the events that unfolded around the investigation.

Following the Civil War, the rural area of Etowah County had several major problems with moonshiners and illicit whiskey stills. At this time, legal whiskey stills were authorized by the government, with revenue from these stills being paid by the operatives to the government. Revenue agents were assigned to different areas to collect taxes and enforce the laws concerning these operations. These officers could close down an operation if these taxes were not paid, and they also had the authority to set the amount of this tax.

The revenue officers assigned to the Etowah County district were actively engaged in an attempt to suppress the illegal distillers during much of the first part of 1875. Officer Peevy was shot during one such confrontation and also had his horse shot from under him. While Officer Peevy was recovering from his wounds, Officer Leatherwood continued his assault on the illegal operations of Etowah County. On May 26, 1875, Officer Leatherwood destroyed the Cooper and Padget stills ten miles west of Van Buren. The following day, Officer Leatherwood would have a date with fate and become part of a mystery that remains unsolved today.

This next day, Revenue Officer Holman Leatherwood visited and had dinner at a still operator's home on Sand Mountain. At this time, this individual was operating one of the government stills in this area. Leatherwood was here to impose the revenue tax on the still or close down this operation. Following the meal at the operator's home, Officer Leatherwood set out to go to the still house and see the operator, who had not been at the family home. Officer Holman Leatherwood would not be seen nor heard from again.

The following morning, James Burgess, who lived about seven miles south of this farm in Big Wills Valley, found Leatherwood's horse standing near his gate as he went out to feed his stock. The saddle and saddlebags were in place but covered with blood. The neck and shoulders of the horse were also covered with blood. Officer Leatherwood's pistol and bowie knife were still in his saddlebags. Mr. Burgess sent to Rodentown for three other revenue agents. These agents came and, with the help of seventy-five people from the surrounding community, found the site of the moonshine still house. On the path leading from the still, two pools of blood were found that were thought to be Officer Leatherwood's. After a two-day search for a body, the hunt was called off.

For several weeks, numerous leads were investigated, with nothing turning up a body. A reward of $8,000 was offered for information in the case of the missing revenue officer. Eventually, a pocket watch was discovered near the still house that was believed to have belonged to Officer Leatherwood. This would lead to several suspects being taken into custody.

Finally, two arrests were made in the case. The two suspects were taken to Huntsville and were eventually bound over for trial by the grand jury. The two defendants were released on $15,000 bail. A break came in the case when a badly decomposed body was found that was identified by Officer Peevy and Leatherwood's father as that of the missing officer. The body was carried to Huntsville, where it was later determined not to be the body of Leatherwood.

The trial eventually took place in Huntsville, with neither defendant being convicted. Although several pieces of evidence were introduced, without a body it was impossible to obtain a conviction.

Several legends have grown from this incident that happened in the Happy Hill area of Etowah County. There were several explanations as to what happened to the body of Revenue Officer Holman Leatherwood, although it was never found. Officer Leatherwood took his place in the pages of Etowah County's history on the early morning of May 27, 1875.

Although many explanations were offered as to the strange disappearance of Officer Leatherwood, very few reasons could be given to the strange happenings at Happy Hill. Occasionally a man has been seen walking the roads in this small suburban area of Etowah County. Strange noises have also been heard here on quiet, late nights, and unusual things have been seen here on nights with a full moon.

For more than 135 years, the "Legend of Happy Hill" has been told and retold. Is this only an urban legend, a story fabricated to be told around a late-night campfire, or is this the account of a revenue agent searching for the one who took his life at such an early age?

The Ghosts of Pulltight

The original survey of the city of Gadsden included the area from First Street to Seventh Street and from Chestnut Street to Locust Street. Although this made Gadsden originally only about seventy-five acres, the town slowly began to move west, north and south. Just west of Gadsden was an area that was originally known by the name of "Pulltight."

Today the Etowah County area is a very safe place to live. The crime rate for our county is low compared to most, and the cities that make up the surrounding area have adequate and able police protection. However, this was not the case during the early days of Etowah County. The early Sheriff's Department, as well as small local police departments, was hampered in enforcing the law. During the late 1800s, there were several areas where the crime rate was extremely high. One such area was Pulltight.

The area of Gadsden that was known as Pulltight was located near the intersection of the "Big Road," which later became known as Twelfth Street, and the Tuscaloosa Road. The Tuscaloosa Road was an early stagecoach route that passed through the Gadsden area. This intersection was once known as Foster's Cross Roads, so named because General Ira Foster had a two-story colonial home on Tuscaloosa, midway between Twelfth Street and Black Creek.

The main part of Pulltight during the 1870s and mid-1880s would later become the home of the Elliott Car Works. This would eventually

Pulltight was the site of many gambling establishments and bawdy houses. This area was cleaned up in the late nineteenth century.

become the site of the Agricola Shopping Center. This community had several saloons and disorderly houses, and crime here was very high. It was almost impossible to police this area because, during the 1880s, the city of Gadsden had a small police department of only twenty-three officers. Twenty-one of these policemen were volunteers and were not paid for their service.

Probably the worst period of Pulltight's long history was between 1882 and 1885, when Etowah County was placed under the prohibition law passed by the state legislature without a vote by the citizens. This was probably the most lawless period in Gadsden's history. The small volunteer band of the Gadsden Police Department made many spectacular raids on several blind tigers operating in the Gadsden area during this time.

During the 1880s, when the railroads came through Gadsden, many of the railroad workers would visit the Pulltight area. These laborers who laid the railroad across Twelfth Street found the places of business at Pulltight to their liking. Most of these workers were rough, tough individuals who drove scrapers and wielded picks and shovels. They shot craps on the ground and on the store porches and played cards out in the open without being bothered by city or county officials. They could also get all the wildcat whiskey they wanted here. One of the more prominent merchants at Pulltight was Andersen Montgomery, a blacksmith who opened a place to eat near his smith to supplement his income.

Eventually, the public outcry became so great and so much pressure was put on the Gadsden Police Department that frequent raids were carried out against the places of business at Pulltight. After a period of time, this area began to slowly see these establishments begin to close.

By 1887, the area known as Pulltight was practically nonexistent. Captain James M. Elliott Jr. purchased much of this land and constructed the Elliott Car Works. This company built and repaired all types of railroad cars. This would become one of Etowah County's largest employers at that time.

For many years, Etowah County had been plagued by several areas of lawlessness. Saloons, blind tigers and gambling establishments had been found in areas like Pulltight. Because of the outcry of many Gadsden citizens, the small police department and the Etowah County Sheriff's Department slowly cleaned out these areas.

Although the bawdy houses and saloons were no longer located here, there was always an eerie feeling that was reported by most people passing this area, especially at night. As tourists were being transported from Noccalula Falls to the riverboat wharf in the late afternoons and early evenings, the horses would always act skittish and hurry past the former location of Pulltight. Later workers at the Elliott Car Works reported hearing strange noises and voices much like a group of people playing cards.

The Ghost of Camp Sibert

The Siberton area of Attalla/Camp Sibert has long been rumored to be haunted. Just when the strange sights and sounds associated with this area of the county first began is not known, although the first sightings began shortly after the closing of this military installation following the end of World War II.

By early 1940, it was beginning to be obvious to most people that the United States was not going to remain neutral in the war raging in Europe. The announcement that a large chemical warfare training facility would be located in Etowah County was made on December 2, 1941, just before

The Gadsden Airport was once part of Camp Sibert. This area has been reported as being haunted by many living in the area.

the Japanese attacked Pearl Harbor on December 7. The army chose a thirty-six-thousand-acre tract of land near Gadsden and Attalla for the training facility.

The Chemical Warfare Training Center was dedicated on December 25, 1942, when the camp was 80 percent complete. The facility cost $16.6 million. In 1943, the camp contained 1,500 buildings and forty-one miles of roads. The camp was between U.S. 411 and U.S. 11 from Big Wills Creek in Attalla to near Ashville in St. Clair County.

The camp was named for General William Luther Sibert, a native of Etowah County and a graduate of the U.S. Military Academy. Sibert had been instrumental in the construction of the Gatum Locks in the Panama Canal.

Camp Sibert at times housed as few as five thousand troops but could accommodate as many as thirty thousand. Camp Sibert also housed a prisoner of war camp that could accommodate up to five hundred POWs.

In the later years of the war, ten members of Hitler's SS troops were held at the camp.

During the years of World War II, several famous entertainers performed at Camp Sibert. Red Skelton and Mickey Rooney were both at Camp Sibert. Joe Louis also fought an exhibition for the troops there.

The camp contributed much to the local economy of Etowah County. Hundreds of civilian jobs were created, and the thousands of men stationed at the camp spent their incomes in Gadsden.

In September 1943, Amelia Harris of the Women's Army Corps arrived to train the first five members of the WAC at Camp Sibert. During the years of the war, both fighter planes and medium-range bombers were housed at Camp Sibert. The installation had a large airfield.

When World War II came to a close, the need for so many military installations also came to an end. Camp Sibert was officially closed on December 31, 1945. The airfield at Camp Sibert was turned over to the city of Gadsden and became the Gadsden Municipal Airport.

Today, the area that housed this giant military facility is an area of farmland and sparsely settled countryside. Most of the indications that this military base once existed long ago have faded into the history of Etowah and St. Clair Counties. What was once part of the base in the mid-1940s turned into blackberry patches in the 1950s and early 1960s, but today it is a growing part of Attalla and Gadsden.

Every now and then, an excited farmer or building contractor uncovers a piece of Camp Sibert in the form of an unexploded mortar or artillery shell—a potentially dangerous relic from our past. Another reminder of Camp Sibert is the legend of an event that supposedly took place there during a late night near the end of the war.

Two Attalla residents were out coon hunting late one night near the military installation when they heard a large truck coming in the distance. The two frightened hunters hid, knowing that they were in an area that was restricted. The truck stopped near where the hunters were hiding, and several armed soldiers forced several men out of the back of the truck. The men were lined up and shot, according to the terrified hunters. The bodies were disposed of, and all evidence of this shooting was cleaned up. Whether this shooting actually took place, or if this is only an urban legend, no records of this execution could ever be found.

Soon all evidence of this giant military installation began to disappear. By the late 1950s and early 1960s, this area was overgrown with blackberries, and the buildings and roads had almost all disappeared.

The area near U.S. Highway 11 has always been a place where some of the ghostly sightings have appeared. A heavy mist has been seen and reported at times in this area. Ghostly specters have also been seen walking in this area where the shootings allegedly took place during the days of the war. Do ghosts of Hitler's notorious SS troops actually walk around Siberton near the place where they were reportedly executed during the final days of World War II?

GIANT FISH, MONSTERS AND UFOs

Most people growing up in Etowah County have heard the strange stories of giant fish in the lakes and rivers of Alabama. Horror stories began to surface during the late 1950s and early 1960s when the many dams were constructed along the Coosa River and the other rivers in Alabama.

These stories of catfish as large as a Volkswagen have been told over and over again for more than fifty years. While these stories have been told as true, is it actually possible for a freshwater Alabama catfish to swallow a man?

The Coosa River is formed at Rome, Georgia, by a junction of the Etowah and Oostanaula Rivers, which flow to Gadsden and on to Wetumpka. Riverboats began bringing commerce to the Etowah County area as early as 1845, when this area was sparsely settled. The steamboats were a major means of transportation for both passengers and goods. As commerce and transportation began, so did the legends of unusual creatures and giant fish.

The stories tell of catfish large enough to swallow a man or at least a small child. These sightings supposedly have come from experienced scuba divers who have witnessed the giants when the structure of the dams have undergone inspection.

Do these sightings explain the story of Jonah in the Bible, which tells of an unwilling prophet who was swallowed by a "great fish," or are they merely products of overly active imaginations? This question seems to appear in the news more frequently in both print and on the Internet, as well as many television specials. There are historical reports that can't be verified from the 1800s and early 1900s of catfish weighing more than two hundred pounds in Alabama. Those may or may not be true. While these fish are huge, and reports of Alabama catfish tipping the scales at one hundred pounds or more surely exist, these fish could not come close to swallowing even a small child. The giants either do not exist or may never be caught if they actually are out there. There are saltwater sea creatures that do exist that could possibly swallow a man whole, including whale sharks and modern-day whales.

Although there has never been any evidence found to support the stories of giant fish in the Coosa River, there has been evidence found throughout much of the world of a prehistoric shark known as megalodon. The giant shark was an ancient relative of the great white shark found throughout much of the world. It grew to seventy-five feet in length and had a mouth large enough to swallow a bass boat! Teeth from the giant were up to seven and a half inches long, and the monster fed on whales. Teeth from the megalodon are found throughout the Southeast.

Reports of strange creatures and giant fish probably will continue to emerge from the Coosa River. The reports have been a part of living in Gadsden and Etowah County as long as people have lived here. Alligators and giant fish also have been seen swimming or floating in the river. An alligator once was reported to have been killed in Town Creek near the Coosa River. During the early 1960s, an alligator reportedly was killed in the lake behind Dwight Mill in Alabama City. A large alligator was also photographed in a farm pond in the Ball Play area near Hokes Bluff.

A giant "monster" terrorized the east Gadsden area during the early 1900s. Reports flourished about a man or manlike creature that stood more than seven and a half feet tall and would wander the streets after sundown, beating anyone it caught outside.

Another legend took place in a neighboring county known as the Choccolocco Monster. It terrorized the people of the area for many weeks until it was exposed as a hoax. It was a local resident dressed in sheets and carrying a cow skull. He would wait behind bushes for oncoming traffic and jump out in the path of the oncoming traffic. The perpetrator would do an eerie dance, usually causing the car or truck to run off the road. The hoax went on for several weeks until the Choccolocco Monster met its match one dark evening. On that night, the monster was waiting for another victim when he saw headlights in the distance. The monster jumped out and started his ghostly dance as the pickup truck ran off the road into the bushes. The driver stepped out of his vehicle with a rifle and opened fire. The monster ran though a barbed wire fence and into history.

Another area terrorized by a "monster" appeared in newspaper reports on January 15, 1891, from Gallant. The account told of a mad beast at large, terrorizing the western portion of Etowah County. On December 25, 1890, the beast attacked a cow belonging to W.B. McClendon, ripping it to shreds. One week later, the creature appeared at the home of G.W. Arnold and attempted to enter the residence. Arnold's dog attacked the beast and was mauled.

The next account was reported one week later. L.D. Brothers was squirrel hunting on the side of Chandler Mountain when he happened upon the creature devouring a sheep. It ran when Brothers released his hounds. The dogs trailed the monster until nightfall, when the hunt was abandoned.

The following morning, a posse formed with more than one hundred heavily armed hunters and hundreds of hounds. The hunters stayed on the trail for days. The beast's ability to devour bone made it almost impossible to pick up a clear trail. Many guesses were made about the type and origin of the beast. Some speculated that it was a lion, a tiger or even a panther. Eventually, the reports of this creature ceased.

Etowah County has always had a rich heritage of UFO sightings. The strange unidentified flying objects have been seen since the 1930s, with many of them being explained or had possible explanations being offered by the United States government.

Since the 1930s, the hum of giant aircraft engines announces the return of one of the Goodyear blimps to the skies of Etowah County. Usually, an air of excitement follows the return of the blimp, with its evening light show and the thundering of its huge motors. Several Goodyear employees are lucky enough during these visits to be selected for a ride on this strange aircraft.

With the coming of the Goodyear Tire and Rubber Company, the blimp soon followed. A giant hangar was built on the Goodyear property behind the plant in east Gadsden to house one of the giant airships when it was in the area or during windy or stormy weather. Another strange aircraft to be seen over Gadsden in the year 1927 was an auto-gyro. This plane was captured on film landing at the old airfield in east Gadsden.

Many UFOs have been reported in the skies over Gadsden. A strange "light show" has been witnessed in the late-night skies looking south from Gadsden toward Southside, an urban area of Etowah County. The sight was described as two large cylindrical objects with flashing red and blue lights traveling back and forth several hundred yards between the two objects. This was reported being observed by many people for several minutes before speeding away silently toward Anniston, Alabama. At the same time, several head of cattle were also reported missing. This strange sighting took place in the early 1970s.

In 1993, a resident of Dog Town, a small rural area, reported being awakened by a strange humming noise and observed a UFO with several lights hovering near the ground. On another occasion, a stealthy aircraft was observed flying over Gadsden. The U.S. Air Force denied the validity of any of these reports. The brow of Lookout Mountain has been a favorite spot to watch for the UFOs that have at times visited the skies over Etowah County.

The Ghost at the Falls

For more than 150 years, the top tourist attraction in Etowah County has been Noccalula Falls. The first people to view this beautiful natural wonder were no doubt the Cherokee Indians living in this area near the falls. The first white settlers in this area during the mid-1800s quickly discovered the natural beauty of the waterfall, and many people believed that the mineral springs located near there had a healing effect on many ailments. Most people living in Gadsden and the surrounding area have heard the legends and stories of the falls for many years. Are these stories factual or are they only urban legends?

One of the first accounts of Black Creek Falls, as it was called back in its early days, appeared in the pages of the *Gadsden Times* in 1869. This account was written by local author and composer Mathilde Bilbro. Ms. Bilbro put in print the story of a beautiful Cherokee Indian princess that had been told for many years. The poem about beautiful Noccalula told of the life and tragic death of one of the area's most famous residents.

Noccalula was the young daughter of a prominent Indian chief living in this area during the late 1700s and early 1800s. Many people believe that this chief was the well-known Cherokee chief Little Turkey. Little Turkey was chief of the great nation located from near Centre, Alabama, in Cherokee County to just below Gadsden. The legend tells that the Indian village was within sight and sound of a great waterfall.

Princess Noccalula was known far and wide for her stunning beauty. Many young Indian braves competed for the hand of the beautiful princess. As the legend goes, Princess Noccalula was in love with a

Noccalula Falls is Etowah County's leading tourist attraction. There have been many tragic accidents in the gorge and creek below.

strong young Indian brave from her own tribe, while her father favored a marriage to a powerful chief from a neighboring tribe. This chief was wealthy and could pay much wampum and horses to the father of Noccalula for his daughter's hand in marriage. Princess Noccalula pleaded with her father to allow her to marry her young brave. The old chief refused and actually had the brave banished from the tribe and driven away. Heartbroken, Noccalula began to make plans to end the marriage that her father had arranged.

On the day of the wedding, a large feast was held. The beautiful Noccalula was dressed in a colorful wedding garment, and the festivities soon began. Princess Noccalula slipped away during the feast unnoticed to put an end to her problem in the only way she knew how. She hurried to the waterfall and walked carefully to the edge of the deep gorge. In an instant she leaped into history and legend. Heartbroken, the old Indian chief gave the name of the gorge and waterfall Noccalula Falls in memory of his beautiful daughter.

In recent years, Indian writings have been discovered on rocks below the falls that give credibility to this legend. Several other Cherokee legends tell of a princess that jumped to her death in a similar manner. These legends have been told from North Carolina to Alabama, although the findings around Noccalula Falls tend to make this the likely place for these events to have unfolded.

For many years, tourists have traveled to Etowah County to view the scenic beauty of the canyon and the falls. Travelers from Rome would take the steamboat to Gadsden to spend the day at the falls. In later years, several businesses and civic leaders recognized the value of this property and encouraged the city to purchase the waterfall and the surrounding lands. Former Gadsden mayor Reuben Mitchell actually purchased the property and kept it in his family until the city was able to purchase the property.

During the early days of the twentieth century, a large dance pavilion was located in the area beneath the falls. While this attraction has been very popular, the creek and waterfall are very dangerous places. Many people have accidentally drowned here during the springtime, when the heavy rains cause the creek to become a rushing white-water creek. Several people have also chosen the bluff to commit suicide. One person determined to end his life here drove an automobile into the gorge, a drop of ninety feet. Many people have slipped into the creek from the wet rocks and drowned when they were swept under the huge rocks by the rushing water.

The waterfall has attracted its share of daredevils for many years. Many high-divers have come to the falls to try their talents against the ninety-foot height and the twenty feet of water in the pool and creek below. Tightrope-walkers have walked high wires here on many occasions.

Noccalula Falls has long been rumored to be haunted. Many people have reported strange feelings and sightings here in the early morning and late evening hours just after sunrise and just before sunset. There is usually an eerie mist associated with the waterfall much like at most waterfalls. Is this beautiful attraction haunted by the ghost of a beautiful Indian maiden who took her own life more than two hundred years ago, or is this gorge haunted by the spirits of one or more of the people who have accidentally drowned here over the years?

The Spirits of Ball Play and Turkey Town

The small rural community known as Ball Play is located in northeastern Etowah County between Hokes Bluff and the Cherokee County town of Centre. This community is at the point where the Ball Play Creek flows into the Coosa River. This area was at one time called Woods Bend.

This section of land was once an important area when the Cherokee and Creek Indian nations were located here. When a controversy would arise between the different Indian tribes, the dispute would be settled in the area known to the Indians as "Ball Play." The men of the tribes would meet on this field and either settle the dispute by fighting or playing a game of ball. The exact type of ballgame that was played here is not exactly known. The game was played with a ball made of animal hides. The exact location of this athletic field is not known, except that it was located next to the Coosa River. On the day of one of these contests, hundreds of members of the two tribes would meet at the field to watch the contest.

One such contest was reported in the *Gadsden Times* on July 7, 1876. This contest had actually taken place in December 1832. At this time, the Creek and Cherokee Indians met on the field at Ball Play to establish a "neutral" territory between the two nations. The land was to be taken from the losing tribe's land. The parcel of land that was at stake was four miles wide and twenty miles long, located on Ball Play Creek. This was an extremely fierce competition, with the Creek Indians winning the contest. Losing the land to the Creeks was a blow to the pride of the Cherokee nation.

Originally, the area known as Ball Play was located in Cherokee County. The first post office was established here in 1840, with John Robinson as the first postmaster. This post office was closed in 1905.

By the mid-1800s, most of the Indians had all but vanished from the Ball Play area. This once important parcel of land would slowly become inhabited by white settlers. Today, very little remains of the influence the Indians had on this area. Occasionally, farmers will find arrowheads and spear points while walking through the freshly plowed fields in and around Ball Play. Relics also turn up on the banks of the creeks and the Coosa River—silent reminders of the great Indian nation that was once located here. Also remaining are the legends of the great ballgames that were held at a forgotten area on the banks of the Coosa River known as Ball Play.

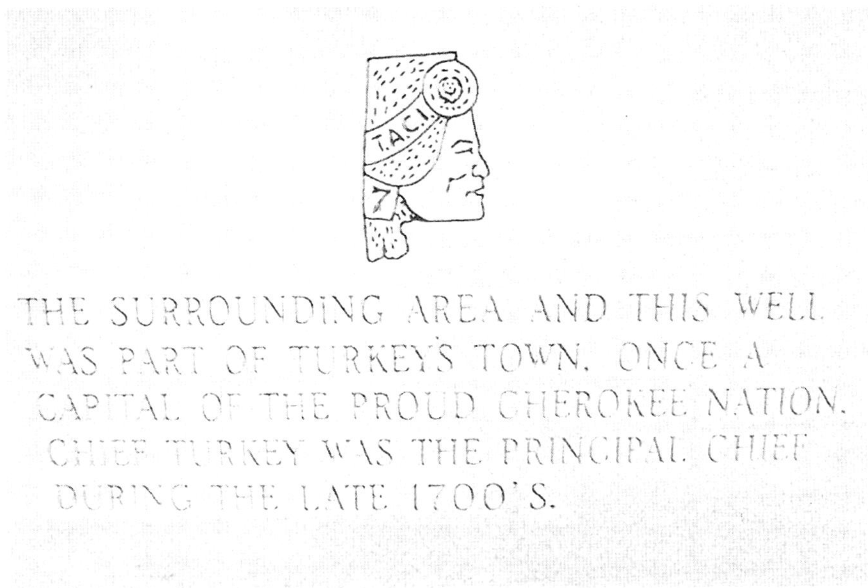

Turkey Town was an important area for the Cherokee nation in Alabama. Turkey Town and Ball Play have been reported as being haunted on many occasions.

Over the years, several businesses have been located in the area. Logging was an important industry here during the early 1900s. Hundreds of acres of timber were cut here and hauled overland to the Coosa River. The timber was then floated downriver to one of the sawmills in Gadsden. Later, more modern means of logging were used when paved roads came to the Ball Play area.

Another industry that was located in the area was a large cotton gin known as Pollards Gin. This gin was important because of the many acres of cotton that were farmed in rural Etowah County. This gin was run by the Pollard family for many years. Over the years, the logging industry and the cotton gins have all but ceased to exist in the Ball Play community. Today this area in rural Etowah County is largely an agricultural area and the home of several large farms and hundreds of Indian legends.

The area of Etowah County that was probably settled first was the community of Turkey Town. This area was the capital of the Cherokee Indian nation as early as 1777. Legendary chief Little Turkey presided over this area, which would come to bear his name as Turkey Town.

According to history, Chief Little Turkey was a strong leader who believed in peaceful village life in addition to bloody raids on opposing Indian villages and whites alike. Indian raids against white settlers were led from the Turkey Town area until 1794, when Chief Little Turkey recognized the inevitable waste of furthering the Cherokee nation's struggle. Before Little Turkey's death in 1818, he negotiated peace with two presidents, Washington and Jefferson. In 1812, he met with General Andrew Jackson and signed an agreement leading to the white settlements of Turkey Town and Ball Play. Stockades were built at Turkey Town in 1837 to protect the Indians from the white settlers, and in 1838 the remaining Indians were sent on the Trail of Tears.

From about 1840 until the mid-1920s, the Turkey Town area was famous for its cotton crops. The red clay fields and the backwaters of the Coosa River made the area an ideal spot for planters.

The location of Turkey Town prompted both the rise and fall of this community. Because of its location on the old route from Chattanooga to Pensacola, settlement in this area was desired by traders and merchants. The old High Town Path also crisscrossed the area. This route connected Atlanta to west Alabama. The location of Turkey Town between Gadsden and Rome proved beneficial for cotton growers in getting their crops to the markets in these two cities.

As the nearby city of Gadsden began to grow, residents of Turkey Town began to move in hopes of landing jobs or opening their own businesses in the fast-growing town. The years of the Depression took a heavy toll on the Turkey Town agricultural economy. The lure of wartime jobs added to the declining population of the Turkey Town area over the next several years.

Over the years, as many as six stores have operated in the Turkey Town area. A cotton gin was also located at Turkey Town, and the Rome–Decatur express made daily stops at the Turkey Town depot. The original church building was a roughly hewn log structure that burned down in 1875.

Today, the small community of Turkey Town, located just north of Gadsden on Highway 411, remains as a quiet reminder of a great Indian nation that once was located in Etowah County. Today the area high atop Lookout Mountain overlooking Turkey Town is overgrown with hedges and brush. This was the spot where Chief Little Turkey would sit to overlook his once powerful Cherokee nation.

Turkey Town today continues its existence as a peaceful farm and cattle community. Old chimneys dot the pastures and sites of old homesteads.

The creeks and streams on which mighty Indian villages thrived still flow, although the Indians were removed more than 160 years ago. Turkey Town was one of the last Indian sites in Alabama.

Legend has it that the original residents of Ball Play and Turkey Town meet on cold winter afternoons to settle the land disputes between the Cherokee and Creek Indian tribes who were removed from this area more than 175 years ago. The ghostly war cries of the games' participants are rumored to still haunt this quiet area of Etowah County.

Concluding Thoughts

For more than 150 years, ghostly sightings and ghost stories have been reported in the Etowah County area. For hundreds of years, ghosts have been reported in writings and literature. Have people actually seen images of spirits or monsters? Have these creatures of all shapes, size and descriptions haunted the earth since man's early beginnings?

Has anyone actually ever seen a ghost? This question will no doubt be debated for the remainder of time itself. Many can attest to the strange occurrences that they have witnessed and to the "unusual feelings" that situations dictate, but do ghosts actually exist? Are there actual exiles from the spirit world that have been sentenced to walk the face of the earth for all eternity, or are these only creations of man's overactive imagination?

Have I ever seen a ghost? The answer is no. I have seen strange things that have taken place at night and felt the odd feelings that come from entering a place that is reported to be haunted. I have felt the cold feeling that supposedly indicates a presence from the spirit world. I have seen things move for no apparent reason, and I have heard noises in older buildings that sound like ghostly, muffled voices in adjoining rooms or coming from an upstairs floor. I have also seen strange orbs of light appear on photographs that were not there when the photos were taken. Other strange occurrences include images that seem to be ghosts that have appeared on photos after the film was developed. I have also witnessed strange things in the night sky that appear to be UFOs, but I have never seen a ghost—only things that I cannot explain.

Do I believe in ghosts? The answer to that question is a resounding "yes!" Ghosts are creations of our own minds and imaginations. We create our own "ghosts" on a regular basis, seeing and hearing things that we want to see and hear. Ghosts can be good or evil, depending on our own mindset. An individual can want to see or hear things so badly that we can eventually condition ourselves to actually see or hear the ghost. On occasion, ghosts have been seen or heard in the Etowah County area that range from helpful to violent. These spirits seem to appear to represent groups of people or individuals from our county's past.

One ghost that has appeared at the Gadsden Public Library on College Street in downtown Gadsden has appeared on several occasions as a helpful spirit. Late one afternoon, two people came to the library to do genealogical research. At this particular time, there was no one available to help the researchers. About an hour passed, and the couple finished and prepared to return home. They were excited to have accomplished so much in a short period of time. When asked by a librarian about their short time in the genealogical files, they replied that they had help from a very experienced genealogist who had shown them how to find things they had been searching for quite some time. The puzzled librarian walked over to the research area, and there was no one there. The librarian went to the couple and asked them to describe who had helped them. The description matched a helpful library patron who had passed away months before.

Recently, when the outbreak of supercell storms and tornadoes tore a path across the South and Southeast, ghostly images were caught on photographs appearing to watch over homes and buildings where large trees had fallen. These images did appear to be the ghostly outline of some type of specter. The images were explained as moisture or dust on the lens of the camera, although the image did not appear on two photographs in succession. These images did not appear on the photos taken inside—only in exterior photos. Are these actually the photos of ghosts watching over the occupants of the dwelling, or are these only optical illusions from advanced digital photography?

Evil or violent ghosts are the ones that appear to frighten individuals or warn of impending danger. Modern-day ghost stories tell of spirits who appear to warn people of bridges being out or trees being down blocking a roadway, often in a frightening manner. Other evil ghosts are the ones that appear as violent spirits and actually strike individuals or throw objects across a room in a building or a house. On one occasion, a medium was brought to Gadsden to investigate possible ghostly or paranormal activity.

At one location, the medium was struck from behind, although there was no one else in the room. This took place in downtown Gadsden and was never explained.

Do ghosts exist? The answer may be "yes," given that they either appear in the imagination of an individual or in the actuality of the people witnessing these strange phenomenon. For more than 150 years, people living in the Etowah County area have seen strange creature, ghostly apparitions and unidentified flying objects. During the 1950s and the Cold War, flying saucers appeared on the horizon for years. The late nineteenth century saw the appearance of sea monsters in the Coosa River, both popular sightings of their times. Are these strange sightings real or only things that we "will" to see?

Many people have attempted to explain some of the strange sightings and unusual occurrences by having people who are experienced in "grave dowsing" come to the area. These people have found unmarked graves and cemeteries that were not even known to exist. While modern science attempts to disprove these practices as hoaxes or as having no scientific basis, these are the only possible explanations other than an overly excited imagination.

During the early hours of the morning, just after midnight, the footsteps of a beloved pet can be heard walking through a dark, quiet house. But this pet has been gone now for several years. Has it returned, or is this only something that the individual wants to see or hear?

About the Author

Mike Goodson has been interested in local history for many years. He grew up in the Alabama City suburb of Gadsden in northeast Alabama and was educated in the public school system of Gadsden. He has been writing and researching local history now for many years.

Goodson writes a history-based column for the *Gadsden Times* that began in 1999 with the "Looking Back" section. Since then, he has written more than six hundred columns relating to local history.

Mike Goodson has authored and coauthored several books on local history and has conducted several local walking tours in downtown Gadsden. He has also conducted a ghost walk and ghost watch downtown during Halloween each year. These have proven to be very popular! He is a lifelong resident of Gadsden and Etowah County. He is married to the former Ann Moore, also a lifelong Gadsden resident.